TAKE TWO

Caroline Thonger (CH) is a technical translator from French and German, and writer of historical non-fiction work *The Banker's Daughter* (Merton Priory Press, 2007) about her German grandmother's family. She was Chief Editor of *Hello Switzerland!* magazine where her articles, investigations and editorials were published. She volunteers with the Geneva Writers Group; her short stories and poems have regularly appeared in the GWG publication *Offshoots*.

With a background in psychology, Vivian Thonger (NZ) is a writer/poet and actor/performer. Her writing has featured online at *Flash Frontier*, *Flash Flood*, short and long lists for NZ's annual Flash Fiction Competition, and has twice won Northland's Short Story prize. Work appears in *Bonsai: Best small stories from Aotearoa New Zealand* (CUP, 2018) and *Te Ripo Wai* (Pavlova Press, 2021); poems are included in eight print editions of *Fast Fibres Poetry*.

Alan Thomas (NZ) is a scientist, sculptor and print artist investigating materiality and dissociations between human perceptions and understandings of the world and what it really might be. *Take Two* is his first foray into illustration.

Take Two is the Thongers' first collaborative project: parallel-writing memories and evidence of their shared past in short, experimental forms. Earlier versions have been long- and shortlisted for the Bath Short Memoir and Reflex Novella prizes.

Take Two

Caroline Thonger
Vivian Thonger

with 20 illustrations by Alan Thomas

CB *editions*

First published in Great Britain in 2023
by CB editions
146 Percy Road London W12 9QL
www.cbeditions.com

© Caroline Thonger and Vivian Thonger, 2023
Illustrations © Alan Thomas, 2023

The right of Caroline Thonger and Vivian Thonger to be identified
as authors of this work has been identified in accordance with
Section 77 of the Copyright, Designs and Patents Act 1988

Printed in England by Imprint Digital, Exeter

ISBN 978-1-909585-54-6

for Tom, Marcus, Sophie, Max, Clio

Acknowledgements

We thank our early readers, encouragers, questioners, shapers and critics:

Shelley Arlidge
Tania Aslund
Dave Borrowdale
Kathy Derrick
Vera Dong
Michelle Elvy
Jac Jenkins
Lynn Jenner
Georgina Lock
Kim Martins
Hazel McCullagh
Catherine Nelson-Pollard
Anna South

We thank Alan Thomas for reading our minds.

Prologue 1

Part One 7

Part Two 75

Part Three 81

Epilogue 137

Postscript 139

Notes 141

PROLOGUE

The first child had a stack of dark hair. Her temperament placid, she ate well and grew fast. Her English relatives saw her as a typical big Thonger and just like her father.

The second child was a screamer, allergic to milk, scowling, blonde. Her German relatives saw her as a typical pale Vollmann and just like her mother.

The older sister grew tall. Asthma kept the younger small. Only 18 months between them.

The mother saw she had a fat child and a sick child. Not the children she'd expected.

The father –

Ursula Thonger, mother and wife

The photo (St John's Wood 1960) shows her about to cross the road, holding her children's hands in a stern grip, forearms surprisingly muscled on her narrow frame. Her voice is loud, her nose big and curved. She's all slamming and rushing: digging tiny plants into the rockery in rageful haste, shaking them pitilessly out of their miniature pots.

She whistles tunelessly, like wind through cracks, or she'll sing a song fragment over and over: 'A tisket a tasket a jolly little basket'.

Her lips, when she goes out, are red and sharp, her handkerchief dotted with lipstick mouths. Her brows are pencilled to match the darkened, permed hairdo sitting high on her head like a helmet.

At home, when the lipstick's worn off, her mouth droops. Except when she's whistling.

They call her Ursel, Ushi, Uzi / often feels woozy / loves her garden
taught not to say pardon / speaks three languages quite perfectly but any deviation / makes her frown in concentration / and force a laugh / not understanding a word / we're used to her phrases and curse words and odd words / *Donnerwetter nochmal* / at the dinner table no banter
no politics no opinion / keeps her peace / anything for a quiet life
our wonderful English guide! enthuse pinned-up postcards / from around the world

Richard Thonger, husband and father

The photo (Mayfair 1960) shows a tall man in a suit: broad shoulders and chest, wide mouth, weak chin. Bald, apart from a neat horsehoe of dark hair around the back of his head. Upright posture. Five-o'clock shadow.

Soft, white hands that wave while he speaks, two fingers nicotine-stained.

Tortoiseshell glasses, less the academic, more the businessman. He rarely takes them off except to massage the dent on the bridge of his nose. The thick left lens is heavy.

In daily life, he lumbers – but when he dances ballroom, he's elegant, sleek, weightless.

He kisses all women on the lips, his daughters too. His speaking voice ranges from baritone to falsetto. He laughs at his own stories. His accent, when not jokey, is Cambridge English.

Kiddiwinks on the blink / me old china rag-and-bone
Froggy onion-seller on yer bike / bonjour cock from Le Continong
down the hatch / where's the catch? / fifteen men on a dead man's
    chest
shysters conmen / bloody good driver / lend us a fiver you old
    skiver
Spanish War fighter / Morse Code writer
all her chums are in cahoots / put in the boot / don't touch my
    papers
sweet-heart poppet moppet / it's *not* an argument say a discussion
don't speak German / only civilised English / how dare you invite
    my child?

Caroline, elder child

In the photo (Puigcerdà 1961), the girl grips the ends of heavy wooden oars. She's midway through the pull, feet braced, teeth clamped onto her lower lip. Her shorts ride up her thighs, bunching around her waist: this is a child – not a young woman – under ten years old. The sunglasses make her appear older: her mother's fashionable, owlish Sophia Lorens.

Despite her father's bulk in the stern, the rowing boat is moving well; strands of hair fly forward, haloing her head. Her pale little sister lazes behind her in the bows, hand trailing in the water. From the stern:

'*Dar*ling! Bring the oars to the middle. Not like that. Straighten up, for goodness' sake. No, Callet, no, no!'

The soft sounds of her name match her
plump cheeks giving smile eager to please
she learned how to write it at the age of three
the curved C a hug a cuddle but when he calls her Callet
it's a whip crack a snap a demand a dagger
more stab words jostling deep inside

Vivian, younger child

She stands still in the photo (Regent's Park 1961), unsmiling. She can't run. She can barely walk without help. At the moment, she can't speak.

In the park, she drops her mother's hand and dashes a few steps, then falls forward in a mock headlong dive.

Hey, there's another inbreath, thanks for showing up! Oh wait, here's an outbreath – go on, use those neck muscles, use every muscle you've got – well, you made a meal out of that one – oh no, d'you mean we have to put up with you going through the whole performance again?

Her sister runs loose, easy circles back to the invalid propping herself up on the grass, their mother reading on a blanket nearby. The older girl flops down. 'Tell me how to run, Weezlewum,' she sings.

'Zigzags,' whispers the girl.

~~convivial~~
~~revivifying~~
surViVor
~~vivacious~~
~~vivid~~

Oma, Ursula's mother

Brussels, Belgium

Smiling, well-dressed. Tiny. Old.

She always puts on jewellery, gloves and a hat when she goes out.

Her heavy coat reaches down to her ankles. It's made from unborn lambs.

She has a Peruvian passport.

Her real name is Eva. She tells everyone to call her Oma. Oma means Grandma in German.

Opa, Ursula's father

Ehrang-Trier, West Germany

Fat. Short. Bald. Old.

He's Dick Vollmann. He's German. His voice is bossy but his English stumbles.

In summer he wears lederhosen.

His wife's name is Ilse. She fusses, but she has nothing to do with us.

PART ONE

April 1953

The White House, Albany Street, London NW1

Dickie,

How ghastly England is! Why on earth did that man have to drag poor Ursel over here when they had a nice life at the Allied Commission in Dusseldorf? Everything is black with filth, and there is hardly room to move in that cramped basement flat with draughty windows and shilling-in-the-slot meters.

Of course times were happier before the war - Ted was a wonderful son-in-law. When I was in London he invited me out to restaurants all the time. I do not suppose this man would ever take me somewhere decent, not that he has even asked me, nor could I bear living near him.

Nevertheless, I cannot let Ursel be without a home, what with the baby. The new lease is in her name so she had better take care of her assets. Otherwise it will all end in tears.

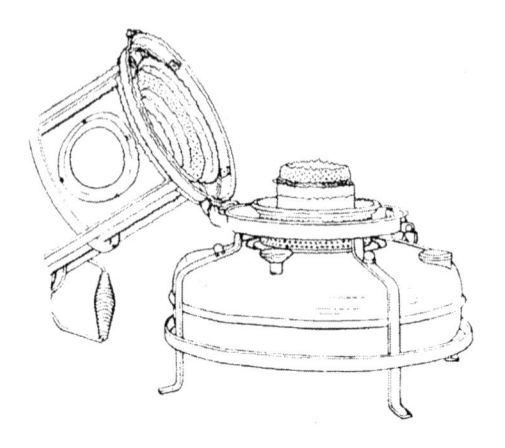

Item 1: Aladdin upright portable paraffin heater
Blue Flame model, green enamel finish

23 Prince Albert Road, London NW1

June 1953

Well-appointed, substantial, end-of-terrace property in late Georgian style situated between Little Venice and Primrose Hill. The house comprises 6 individual flats on three floors, producing a potential income of circa £1,638 per calendar year minus expenses. Rates for the entire building: £305 per annum; water rates £50 per annum. Potential for landlord and family to occupy one flat while renting out the other five as a useful source of income.

Habitation
Basement flat
2 First Floor flats
Zoo flat
Balcony flat
Cottage flat (in small building in the walled garden)

Each self-contained flat is equipped with tap (running water), solid-fuel stove, electric lighting and an individual coal fire. Most have a private water closet. Coal can be delivered to and accessed via the coal chute close to the basement flat. Capacity for gas installation in whole house.

The property stands on the main arterial road leading to London's West End. The nearest 274 bus stop is a short walk away at Primrose Hill. Lord's Cricket Ground, St John's Wood and Hampstead are nearby, while Regent's Park and the Zoological Gardens can be easily accessed on foot.

Asking price for 99-year lease: £5,000.

Boy

Primrose Hill, London NW1

The boy goes up and down the slide, humming to himself. He wears grey trousers, a grey belted raincoat, and a grey cap.

From the sandpit, I watch him go up and down, up and down. On the bench, my mother chats to the woman in brown next to her. Vivvy kicks her feet up. She's strapped into the pushchair and Mum won't let her out.

I pat sand down flat with my spade and tip the bucket upside-down. The castle comes out wonky because this sand is dry and gritty, not like at the seaside.

The boy stands rigid in the sandpit, staring at me. He has stopped humming and doesn't blink.

'Hello,' I say. 'I go to big school. Do you want to play with me?'

There's no smile. The boy moves closer; the grown-ups stop talking. The woman next to my mother shouts, 'No, Simon!'

She springs to her feet, takes the boy by the arm and leads him back to the slide. He goes up and down, up and down. I start to go after him.

Mum calls me back. 'Come on, Caroline, we're going home.'

Vivvy lets out a *'mmpf'* of frustration. Soon I'm trotting to keep up, away from Primrose Hill and across Albert Terrace.

Cursing under her breath, Mum bumps the pushchair down the uneven stone steps to our basement flat. I ask, 'Mummy, why couldn't I play with that boy?'

She replies at once, not looking at me. 'His nanny said he strangles little girls.'

I'd wanted to play with him.

Before pushing the door open, Mum turns around. Her face softens. 'I said, he throws *sand* at little girls.'

Grandmother's footsteps

23 Prince Albert Road

The Zoo is opposite our house. At dawn, things moan and howl.

Once, from our upstairs window, I watch a keeper walk a rhinoceros on a lead, like a dog. The immense head sways and each splayed foot spreads as it takes the animal's weight. The one eye I can see resembles my grandmother's: buried in wrinkles.

Now, every night, I'm running from an enraged rhino, huffing and slobbering closer. I scrabble into a crack, curl up, squeeze eyes shut, will myself to disappear.

Sensing a presence, I stop breathing. Must look.

A gleam.

Millimetres above me, a monstrous eye presses to the crack.

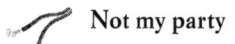

Not my party
Soundtrack: 'Dicky Bird Hop' sung by Ann Stephens

23 Prince Albert Road

The petticoat with three hoops makes my dress balloon out. Pretty as a little princess.

We're about to leave, as Tante Plinter comes into the kitchen. My mother beams and points at me.
'Do you like my party outfit?' I ask, twirling this way and that for Plinter.

With a startling flourish, she lifts her tweed skirt. Her beige stocking is held up by something like a pulley or hook; the top of the stocking is rucked and saggy. I see mottled skin.

Bending down, her face close to mine, she screeches, 'Do you like my suspender belt?'

They're both laughing. I want to take my dress off and run away.

Item 2: Grundig 5050/3D 1954 table-model radio
(short/long/medium wave), wood surround,
with feet, fabric-wound flex

No-girl

23 Prince Albert Road

She hadn't wanted to go for a walk with her grandmother. They'd got as far as the middle of the zebra crossing when the girl lay down.

Her grandmother had cajoled, begged, yelled, 'Get up, stop screaming, you'll be run over by a lorry!' and finally clutched at a stranger to drag the child out of the road. On her back on the cold tarmac, the girl had felt a fierce thrill as traffic screeched to a stop.

Back indoors, told to sit on the sofa, she could still hear the traffic. Her grandmother, frowning, came to sit next to her. She frowned back and shut her mouth tight to keep in the word that always wanted to leap out: No.

'I'm going to tell you a story,' said her grandmother, her voice light. The girl had expected a reprimand or smack. Stories were for bedtime. The old lady continued, 'Once upon a time, there was a little no-girl – isn't that funny? Imagine, a girl who says no all the time – eat your dinner: no! Kiss your Tante Plinter: no! Always no. Wasn't she a silly? Something bad would surely happen.'

The child sat still, waiting.

'A genie heard about the little no-girl and he came to see for himself. No this, no that – and what a grumpy face! – she made the genie so cross. He threw magic dust over her and shouted, Now you must say no, forever. To break the spell, the only way is to look for me in the Deep Dark Forest.'
A shiver trickled along the girl's spine.

'Well, the no-girl grew up and one day, a prince rode by on his white horse. Would you like to ride with me? he asked: no! She loved horses but she could only say no. How she cried. Another prince came from the spice lands and he said, Will you come on faraway adventures with me? No! And a third prince fell in love with her long hair. Will you marry me? he asked: no!

'And at last, she ran away into the Deep Dark Forest to look for the genie. I wonder if she ever found him? Was the spell broken? What happened to her? We can imagine, can't we?'

The old woman was whispering now, her face close to the girl's.

Dusk had fallen and the room was dim. The girl forced herself to look away from her grandmother's grimace, her teeth, and knew in the pit of her stomach that the no-girl was still out there, still searching.

The kitchen door clattered open and her mother shouted over the radio: bread and jam for tea? 'No,' said the child in a small voice.

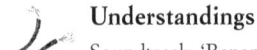

Understandings
Soundtrack: 'Banana Boat (Day O)' sung by Harry Belafonte

23 Prince Albert Road

At bathtime, we wrestle our silverback.
His hefty shoulders shed warm-water cascades.
We squeal and commandeer his shaggy bulk
sloshing us from ship to shore. Seaweedy pelt,
mounded rounds of belly roll. We eel-slippery slips
mountaineer, shampoo his bristly knees with Matey,
get lost in armpit caves. He rests, our ears pressed
to his furred chest, tuned in to his heart's slow drum,
rumble and hum –
and we scramble clear, dripping,
when her footsteps skip upstairs.

Item 3: Gentleman's shaving set: leather case, badger-hair brush,
straight razor, pot of cream, 4711 cologne

Lift-off

Andernos-les-Bains, Gironde, France

Stork-legged, local children scour the surf in the early morning sun. Jagged pincers wave from plastic buckets; I don't dare pick up a live crab.

A group of us waits for Le Chef on a wooden pontoon floating in shallow water. Seaweed and barnacles encrust the edges; fish smells rise from wet wood. An old tyre hangs from a rusty metal arm.

Our swimming lessons don't vary: we take turns with the tyre in the warm sea, while Le Chef uses the metal arm to swing us about. He yells instructions: *'Comme une grenouille, Lucien! Respire, Didier, respire!'* He makes us laugh, in his matelot hat.

Today, the tyre has gone. Le Chef picks up the boys, one after the other, and throws them into the water. Like they're flying. I'm excited for my turn.

My belly yaws; I'm flailing in air; I'm floating on the waves. It's better than swings or slides, better than holding a live crab.

'Look at me, Vivvy!' I shout as I kick my arms and legs. 'I'm swimming, I'm swimming!'

But they're all back at the beach villa. Nobody's watching.

Summer

Andernos-les-Bains

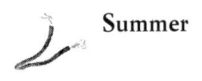

As if I've stepped on an overripe fig. Dark red wells up from an oozing fissure that's appeared in my grimy big toe, spreads out over my foot, seeps into the white dust I'm covered in.

Dazzled by the white road, white gravel, my sister's white sunhat ahead of me, I stumbled.

She turns and comes back, tries to lift me, but I'm heavy and screaming. Her pale primrose blouse, pearl buttons, round collar. Our pink-striped seersucker shorts, wide-legged. Later, my leather sandal, stiff with dried blood. I won't put it back on.

Catching crabs

Andernos-les-Bains

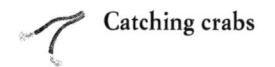

We wade through warm wavelets. Behind us, tiny figures. Mum and the picnic; Dad, a mound on a towel.

'What's that white line?' asks Viv, pointing ahead.
'That's where the big waves live,' I tell her.
'Can we go there?'

I take her hand and stride forward, the sea knee-deep, ribbed sand underfoot, hot sun on my back.

Something hard and scratchy scuttles under my toes. I drop Viv's hand, stumble into a sunken crater, go under. The sand slides away and Viv tumbles into me, squashing me down. Her feet kick against my body as she begins to climb.

Her legs are around my neck and she clings to my head, forcing me further downward and herself above the water. The sand won't let me find my feet.

For a second my head breaks the surface. I take a gasping breath and swallow seawater, rolling under again. I yank at her feet, try to dislodge her octopus-like grip, and then she's gone.

A thick arm has grabbed me by the waist and is lugging me upwards. My eyes are shut tight, but there's a burst of light, a confusion of bubbles.

A man has dumped us both on the beach. For a moment we stand, spitting and retching. My mouth is so salty. Viv's arms are wrapped around my middle.

'C'est à vous, ça, M'dame?' the man shouts to our mother.

'Ah, mon Dieu – merci, monsieur!' She doesn't move from the picnic blanket; she holds out a towel.

Bedraggled, we clamber up the beach together. Viv still hasn't let go.

'Vivvy pushed me under the water.' My voice is trembling. 'She drowned me.'

My mother is busy drying Viv's plaits.

I sit on the blanket. I look over to Dad – asleep.

Item 4: Steiff mohair-plush toy tiger, recumbent, hand stitching, green glass eyes, size of a small cat

Drag

Littlehampton, West Sussex, England

A poster in the foyer announced the hotel's fancy-dress party that evening. Racks of costumes stood ready for guests. After breakfast, Caro and I were feeling our way along feather boas and satin dresses when Dad called us away.

'But I want to be a fairy,' said Caro.
'And I want to be a ladybird,' I said.
'Yes, but I'll make much better outfits, you'll just have to stand still for a bit,' he said. 'I've been to the shop.' He held up a roll of brown paper, string, glue, packets of hair grips, and bustled us upstairs.

We stood in our room all day, the pale seaside light slowly fading to grey. Hair pinned flat against our heads, our scalps and legs ached. I looked at Caro: over white vest and pants, she was draped to her knees in brown paper scrawled with fleur-de-lys designs. I suspected I must look the same. Now Dad was fastening lopsided caps – red felt glued to cardboard – onto our sore heads, swearing under his breath, his cigarette smouldering in the ashtray.

Mum had been out for a long beach walk; her cheeks were pink from the icy wind. She was lying on the bed with a magazine, ignoring us. Her gypsy skirt lay beside her. 'Do as you're told,' she mouthed when I caught her eye. A clock ticked.

Downstairs, the staff moved furniture for the big buffet.

I rubbed my stomach and Caro rubbed hers back; the brown paper crinkled and crunched against our string belts. We'd stopped giggling hours ago.

At last, when Dad stood us against the wall to take a photo with the Box Brownie, he beamed.

'What a triumph! They'll never know,' he said. 'We'll need names.'

Our mother said nothing, humming as she put on her lipstick.

Rustling our way down the main staircase, we heard the clink of cutlery on china. Late. When we ventured in, dozens of elegantly costumed diners looked up from their plates. Caro and I stuck close together. Dad pushed us forward.

'Meet Bedivere and Gawain, twin pageboys to King Arthur,' he announced.
'Twins?' said an elderly guest. 'More like Laurel and Hardy.'

People stopped eating to laugh.

I closed my eyes and imagined easing out the hateful hair grips one by one. And stabbing them into every plateful of turkey breasts and thighs.

Persuasion

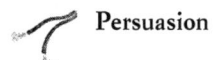

Avenue Armand Huysmans, Brussels, Belgium

'Come, child.' Oma glowers down at me, holding out her gloved hand. 'We'll take the tram.'

My mother arranged this first visit to Brussels. As soon she spied my grandmother coming in through the airport's glass doors, she dropped my little suitcase by my feet, gave me a peck on the cheek and went back inside. She turned once to wave. I'd thought the three of us were staying together.

Now I'm running along with my grandmother, who has me in one hand while I grip my suitcase in the other. Her chic hat matches her Persian lamb coat.

Clanking and squealing, the dark-green tram appears. Its silvery rails snake along the middle of the road. I have my first encounter with the citizens of Brussels: at first nobody offers their seat to the white-haired lady. She glares wordlessly at a young man, who reluctantly stands up. The seat is hard and made of wood; my suitcase is wedged on my lap. We change trams twice. The streets are cobbled. My grandmother's court shoes click over uneven paving stones.

'Vous faites des grimaces, Madame,' announces a hefty woman waiting for us in Oma's first-floor apartment. This is Louise, my grandmother's home help. She's Flemish. My grandmother does indeed make funny faces sometimes, but I have been strictly brought up not to make personal remarks.

The flat is perfectly tidy. All the furniture must be antique. In the sitting room are severe sofas and chairs, gold-framed portraits, ornate rugs, a writing bureau. We don't go into the dark dining room.

There are no picture-books, toys or games. I promise myself I won't knock anything over. My bed is so high that I need a chair to climb into it. The old oaken wardrobe smells of mothballs. Why has Mum sent me here? I miss my sister.

Oma has *Graubrot* and *Leberwurst* for breakfast; I have a *petit pain au chocolat*. We save every crumb for the sparrows chirruping on the balcony. I worry about the sputtering gas-ring, and the wobbly coffee-pot. For long hours, Oma sits at her bureau and writes letters. On good days we walk across the road to the little park bursting with crocuses, and feed the ducks.

One day my grandfather comes to lunch, all the way from Germany. Before he arrives, Oma makes me sit at the kitchen table, while she brushes my short dark hair too hard. 'We have to make them glossy for your grandfather, don't we?' she says, while I try not to wince. I don't know who 'they' are.

Opa doesn't live with Oma. He interrogates me about school, and I show him my best handwriting. Later he pats me on the head, and then begins to snore in the armchair. The newspaper slips down his round belly and falls onto the floor.

'Go and pick up the paper,' Oma whispers to me.
'But Oma, that's not fair,' I reply. 'Opa dropped the paper – he should pick it up.'
'Pick up the newspaper,' Oma says again.

I refuse to back down.

My grandmother leaves the room. I find her talking to Louise in the kitchen. As I come in she says, 'I wonder what *this* tastes like?'

On the table is the most mouth-watering cake. Lemon-scented; covered in icing; decorated with an artistic chocolate swirl.

Oma turns to me and smiles. 'Pick up the paper, Caroline.'

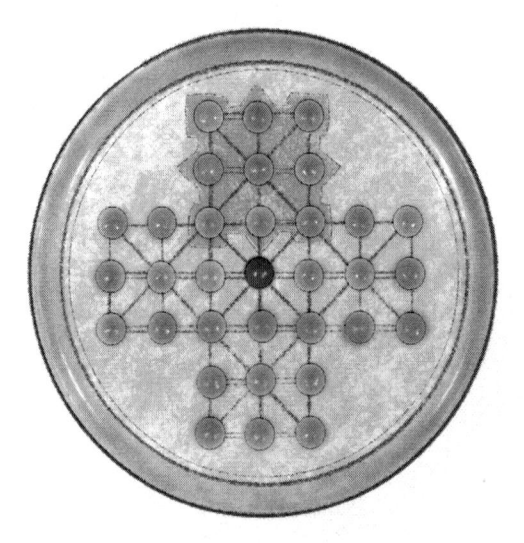

Item 5: Circular hand-carved walnut-wood solitaire board, dimpled; antique marbles

My heart leaps up

Grasmere, Westmorland, England

Yesterday, on Loughrigg, Dad stopped reciting Wordsworth to unzip his anorak and rub his hand across his chest. An ambulance took him to Carlisle, the nearest hospital to the Lakes. Mum says we'll be allowed to visit in a few days.

Out in the cold conservatory at the back of the Rothay Hotel, I'm colouring in the line drawings of my *Living Things for Lively Youngsters* book. I'm sure that I'm exactly one of those lively youngsters, and I intend to use my 72-shade Rowney pencil set to bring every page to life. The river in spate hurtles past in watery spring sunshine. I use four different purples on the cross-section of the heart.

Caro comes out to sit next to me and points to the word 'chambers' describing the four compartments.

Then we move on to the heron.

Prickly

Marbella, Andalucia, Spain

Fine sand blows over the stone slabs. It's hot, the Spanish hills crackling with cicadas. Lunch tables covered by checked peasant tablecloths stand in the shade of a rampant vine.

My bare legs stick to the chair. Mum's cotton skirt billows around her legs. We eat our tomato salad in silence, while Dad keeps rearranging the oil and vinegar bottles, the salt and pepper shakers, the heavy silver cutlery.

They start a conversation.

Dad: 'We'll go for a drive this afternoon, so let's look at the map.'
Mum: 'I haven't got it.'
Dad: 'Yes, you have. I distinctly remember you had it. So where is it?'
Mum: 'I think it's in the brown bag.'
Dad: 'What brown bag? We don't have a brown bag.'
Mum: 'You know, the brown bag.'
Dad: 'Brown bag, brown bag, *what* brown bag?'
Mum: 'The brown bag, Richard.'
Dad: 'What are you talking about? There isn't a brown bag.'
Mum: 'But we brought it with us – '
Dad: '*What brown bag?*'
Mum: 'The brown bag in the bedroom – '
Dad: '*What brown* – ? Oh, you mean the SUEDE bag.'
Mum: 'That's what I said, the brown bag.'
Dad: 'For God's sake, why can't you call things by their proper names? It's a *suede* bag.'

He scrapes his chair back noisily, hurls his napkin onto the table, and stalks into the hotel. Waiters and guests are staring. Mum gazes at the hills. I swing my legs, eyes down. The cicadas crackle.

November 1960
Soundtrack: 'Das ist die Berliner Luft' sung by Lizzy Waldmüller

23 Prince Albert Road

Dickie,

My impression of that man remains unchanged. He is disagreeable, stupid, small-minded, and pig-headed. He knows everything better, has a great desire to show off, lacks sincerity - and worst of all, he is colossally conceited.

He is like a fat parasite, getting under Ursel's feet, doing nothing all day long. Is he expecting me to keep him forever?

After forking out for the next new house, I have had it! Ursel will never again receive money from me.

32A Wildwood Road, London NW11

December 1960

Generous, detached family residence on one-third of an acre, and an unimpeded view of the unspoiled Heath Extension. Attractive L-shaped construction in red herringbone brick, featuring elegant sash windows, ornamental shutters, and balcony above the entrance porch. This exceptional neo-Georgian home forms part of Hampstead Garden Suburb and enjoys all the benefits of the eastern end of the development.

The property comprises 5 bedrooms, 4 bathroom/cloakrooms, 2 reception rooms, kitchen, study, attic space. The spacious hallway features a high-quality parquet floor and impressive broad staircase. Beyond the kitchen the ground floor includes compact staff quarters. Potential for central heating to be installed.

The main entrance is accessed through a gate in the front garden, which includes a driveway leading to the garage (space for 2 family cars).

The rear garden comprises a small orchard, a greenhouse, a fruit-and-vegetable growing section with raspberry canes and asparagus, and lawn.

Asking price: £15,000.

Crossing over

Wildwood Road

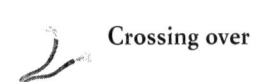

It's the road I notice first: smooth, clean asphalt without markings. Then, the quiet.

We're parked opposite a pair of stone gateposts, a dark holly hedge and a red brick house with a row of tall windows like big, blank eyes.

'Girls, imagine living here!' Dad's fag points jauntily upwards.

'Mmm.' Noncommittal.

Mum twists in her seat to face us. 'It's got much more room, and isn't the garden – '

Dad interrupts. 'Well anyway, sausages, this is our new home.'

He's wrong. Home is our city house hugged up against a jumble of others. Home is the noisy, grinding main road outside, flanked by crusty pavements dotted with yellow-and-brown cigarette butts; the oil-slick surface, black with coal dust, glittering with crushed glass. Coal trucks, buses and lorries. Home is my tin of flattened treasures: bottle tops, feathers, a paper-thin mouse.

We move. I mourn indoors.

One afternoon, my tin of treasures left unopened, Caro and I hold hands and cross the road. On the other side, we run down a footpath meandering through tall grass, towards trees. We walk on. When we turn back, the house and its eyes have disappeared.

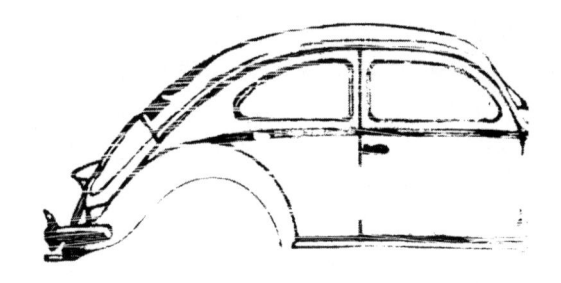

Item 6: Baby-blue Volkswagen Beetle, 2-door, chrome fittings, reg. TMP 66

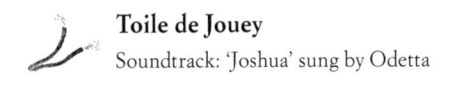

Toile de Jouey
Soundtrack: 'Joshua' sung by Odetta

32A Wildwood Road

Tell you about picking my way down the joins, rubbing small blisters where air was trapped behind the wallpaper, that poor stale air.

Tell you about the pattern, repeating imaginary countryside scenes. Monochrome-printed in brown, on a cream background. Pairs of pheasants and lolling lovers and hay bundles, cows and cottages, over and over, all the sickening way up the walls.

Tell you about the bucolic cluster closest to my face that I rubbed and picked and licked until only dirty peasant ghosts were left. Paper and glue and plaster worried away. Me worried I'd be punished. Tried to draw them back in brown pencil and my hand shook. It always did. The asthma pills did it. And they didn't do anything.

Tell you no one noticed that patch of wallpaper. I was always in front of it. Always ill in bed.

Tell you the cock-eyed pheasants never looked right again.

Tell you they started looking at me.

February 1962

Ehrang-Trier

Evie,

It is incomprehensible why Ursel cannot assert herself when it comes to the health of her daughter.

Like a child, she has to ask her husband's permission for everything. The man has realised that he will always have money, so what else could he want? You have been too generous. He is a pig.

Her shoes I

32A Wildwood Road

Open the mirrored white wardrobe and a waft of secret mother escapes: Coty face powder, lipstick, remnants of Chanel No 5. Unlace the twin velvet shoe bags. Small feet slide into two-tone, navy-and-white pumps, delicate filigreed holes punched along the seams. Teetering across the bedroom carpet, dragging the shoes on outstretched toes, trying on a voice to match: 'How *do* you *do*?' Friction burns soles, and guilt rises as a key clatters in the front-door lock.

Four-and-twenty blackbirds

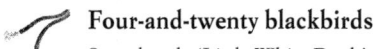

Soundtrack: 'Little White Duck' sung by Burl Ives

32A Wildwood Road

My mother takes down a cookery book.

'You can read out the recipe for me,' she says, finding the right page.
'Can't we have baked spaghetti?' I say, making a face.
'We like goulash, don't we? This is the same, with a bit of pastry on top. It'll be lovely.'

First, we make the stew: carrots and onions and meat. Mum uses the grater, instead of chopping the vegetables into cubes.

'Mum, you're doing it wrong,' I say.
'Nonsense!' She clamps a saucepan lid down on the frying pan.

Now we're onto the pastry. She hacks up a whole packet of Anchor butter with a carving knife, and tips it into the big bowl of flour.

'But butter isn't – ' I object, my finger on the recipe.
'Lard is what common people use,' she says. '*We* have butter.'

After a lot of sticking to the rolling pin, there's a flattish round of yellow pastry on the worktop. Mum's apron is covered in grease, the floor spattered in flour. She ladles the contents of the frying pan into a Pyrex dish, puts an egg-cup upside-down in the middle, and slaps the pastry on top. The oven timer is set.

In my head I'm watching the construction of an apple pie in my best friend Jackie's tiny kitchen. How her mum's fingers crimp neat edges like a scallop shell; how she cuts pastry diamonds to decorate the top; how she brushes the pie with egg to make it shiny.

No scallops or diamonds on my mother's version.

'What's for supper then?' says Dad, emerging from his study.
'It's what you asked for,' says Mum grandly. 'Steak and kidney pie.'

Dad eyes the dish steaming on the table. 'Are you mad?'

The egg-cup has tipped over during baking, and most of the pastry has gone down with it. Pale, sunken lumps contrast with a few burnt remnants clinging to the edge of the dish; insipid liquid seeps upwards.

'You haven't the slightest bloody idea how to make a decent English pie,' says Dad.
'Well, it all tastes the same, doesn't it?' says Mum.

Dad leaves the table to clatter about in the larder.

Mum hands out the bowls. Viv's eyes meet mine, across the table. Dad makes himself a plate of bread and cheese.

Item 7: Mouli mechanical food grinder and puree-maker, metal, well-used

Word

Hampstead Way, London NW11

'Ullo darling, like me winkle pickers?' The tall boy leers in my direction.
'Mmm,' I respond, not knowing what to look at. His mates laugh raucously from the bench, as he swaggers back to them.

It was a Saturday morning and Mum had deposited us at the playground at the far end of the Heath extension, before driving off to the Golders Green shops. As usual I was left in charge of my little sister. We took turns on the slide, and spun the roundabout without getting on. I left Viv on the swings and wandered over to the sandpit, which had a nearby bench for mothers and nannies to watch over their charges.

A trio of boys appeared, much bigger than me, perhaps as old as 13. They squatted on the back of the bench, and passed a packet around. One of them vaulted down and sauntered towards me. His quiff of blond hair stuck up like a rhino horn.
'Fancy Teddy Boys, do ya?' said the boy. Acutely aware of my oh-so-short, pudding-bowl haircut and tomboyish dungarees, I straightened up to meet his gaze.

I spot the Beetle parked on the kerb.
'Hey, doll, wanna fuck-up?' shouts the boy from the bench. More laughter.
Mum is waving her gloved hand impatiently.

'Come on, Viv, Mum's here,' I call over to the swings. When I look back, the boys have vanished.

On the short drive home, my curiosity overtakes me.
'Mum,' I say from the front seat, 'why are they called Teddy Boys?'

Hearing no reply, I plough on. 'And what's winkle pickers?'
Viv sniggers from the back of the car. Mum ignores me, concentrating on driving.
'And what's a fuck-up?' I rush on.

She grips the steering wheel hard, and stamps on the brake. We lurch forward again, as she grinds the gears.
'*Ca*roline,' she says, spitting my name out like a cough. 'Ca-ro-line, don't you *ever* use that word!'

Parking the car in the drive, Mum grabs the shopping basket from under the bonnet and bustles towards the front door. We're left trailing in her wake.

'What word?' I hiss, pushing Viv upstairs towards our attic playroom.
'Winkle picker?' she hisses back.

March 1962

Brussels

Dickie,

I am filled with dread. My Carolinchen - this concerns me the most - will be sacrificed to the sickly younger sister.

Everything seems black to me - really black.

Letter home
[translated from German, from the live-in au pair]
Soundtrack: 'De Hamborger Veermaster' sung by Freddy

32A Wildwood Road

23 May

Dearest Mutti,

I followed Mr Thonger's instructions from the Dover ferryboat all the way into London. The city is stuffed full of thousands of people rushing about, and so many cars, the traffic is crazy! I saw my first double-decker buses, three in a row, and black taxis, and a red letterbox, just like the pictures in our English schoolbooks. I tried to call the number from a phone box - it was difficult with Button A and Button B, but a station guard helped me use my English pennies. When the bus got to the Hampstead bus-stop, there was Mrs Thonger to meet me with the little girls.

Oh Mutti, they are adorable: Caroline is 10, with short hair, big eyes and a lovely smile. Vivian is 8, very small and shy with me. They live in a mansion next to a parkland called Hampstead Heath (I can't pronounce it yet!). I have my own bedroom, and I'm invited to join the family in the kitchen for breakfast and the evening meal. Mrs Thonger says she will show me how to cook for the girls when she and Mr Thonger go out. On the first night we had lamb chops and fried potatoes - Mutti: lamb is delicious!

The family are not like anyone we know in Emsdorf. Mrs Thonger is out all day, taking tourists around London on a coach. Mr Thonger sits in his small study downstairs. He also plays the piano without music. I try not to laugh when he leans close and opens his mouth wide to show me how to pronounce English. I hope I'm remembering my manners. In my spare time, I go to a language school in Golders Green. If only I'm brave enough to explore all the museums on my own!

There's something I must ask you. Last night I was woken up by a thudding sound. At first, I thought it was in the front bedroom where Mr and Mrs Thonger sleep (sorry to mention such a thing!). But then it seemed one of the girls was jumping on her bed, in the middle of the night!

Mutti, if it happens again, should I say something to Mrs Thonger? Write soon!

A big hug from your daughter, Gerda

Headbangers

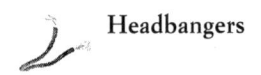

32A Wildwood Road

It helped us get to sleep, we both did it: bumping.

Bumping by moonlight, bumping my sheets, blanket and eiderdown off, bumping my bedstead against the wall, bumping my bed across the room, bumping my head sore and myself into breathlessness – pausing, and hearing my sister bumping on the other side of the landing, and feeling comforted, and trying to find a bit of my skull that wasn't sore and bump with that. It gave me asthma; it soothed my asthma.

According to the *Journal of Clinical Sleep Medicine*, Sleep-related Rhythmic Movement Disorder (SRRMD) is relatively common in young children. In our family, only our mother had her sleep disrupted, getting up every night to pull us away from the headboards, to tuck us back in tightly. There is some evidence that children with RMD have higher anxiety levels. The disorder is rarely reported among adults.

I was the only one of us two to suck my thumb and bite my nails to the quick; my mother dabbed on Bitex for a few months but I kept on biting, kept on sucking, shuddering with the bitterness.

I still bite my nails.

My sister still bumps.

Shipshape

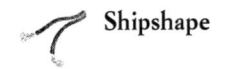

32A Wildwood Road

'I've got a job for you, Podge,' says Dad from the landing. 'Come on, help me sort my socks.'

I go into his dressing-room. There's a pile of socks on the floor. I sit cross-legged beside them.

'Let me show you,' says Dad, sitting down on the bed.

He lays two socks together on the bedspread, folds the top one back half-way, and then somehow inserts that sock into the sock underneath, giving it a trim cuff with the feet pressed precisely together.

I pair up two socks beside me. He snatches them out of my hand.

'No, no, *no*, not like that, Callet!' he says. 'Can't you see, these don't even match.'

The two socks seem like a pair. This one: a dark-green pattern with a faint red stripe. And that one: a dark-red pattern with a faint green stripe.

Dad puts his own folded socks away in one of the drawers, as straight as soldiers standing to attention. I've assembled three pairs. He whines in exasperation and pulls me up onto the bed, his weight tipping me close to him.

His face is so glum.

'Now listen to me Callet,' he says. 'I have to tell you something that you won't believe. You see, when I was a boy, I was clumsy. Yes, *clumsy*.'

I don't know if we're talking about socks anymore. Something sharp turns over inside me.

43

'What you have to realise, Callet,' he goes on, 'is that *you're* clumsy too. It's something you have to live with. *If* you're very lucky, you might grow out of it.'

I reach for more socks, making sure I have two *exactly* matching ones.

February 1963

Ehrang-Trier

```
Ursel,
    What is binding you to this man? Why do you fear
that he would be given custody of the children should
you get divorced? What does he know about you? I am
well aware how much you have enjoyed the attention of
men. Has this continued outside your marriage, giving
him grounds to blackmail you? You can write openly to
me; you know I understand. But I cannot understand
your indifference to your fate and the fate of your
children.
```

I fear Mamma's spiteful tongue, her revulsion for things that can't be helped, like my eye.
I fear my younger sister's sulky face, her eternal coldness; she may never forgive me.
I fear my elder sister might withdraw her warmth.
I fear my brothers' rages; they are not susceptible to reason.

Precious

32A Wildwood Road

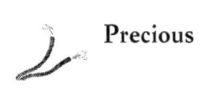

We avoided the cat-pissy part of the garden under the overgrown hedge, cackling with magpies – except for the day Caro spotted a fledgling blackbird shivering on bare earth: yellow-rimmed beak and fluffed feathers. We settled it into a leaf nest in the corner of a cardboard box.

We stowed the box under the hedge and kneeled next to it to shoo away the neighbour's cat when she came too close. 'Our secret brother,' whispered Caro, stroking the soft feathers. 'No one can steal you.'

The hedge above us swayed and a face appeared. Dad. I wrapped my arms around the box.

'What've you found?' Before we could answer, he crouched down and grabbed the chick in one big hand.

The bird struggled, freeing one wing; the other hung at the wrong angle. I yelped.

Dad snorted. 'D'you know how to help him?'
We shook our heads.

He glanced at Caro. 'Right, we'll make a splint out of that.' He pointed to the side of her head.

I disentangled her hair slide. Caro handed it to him slowly: it was a present from Oma. We kept quiet while he fumbled to clasp the flexible metal halves over the wing joint, the bird flapping non-stop.

'Perfect fit,' said Dad, a bit out of breath. He rubbed his head. 'Time for a cigarette.'

The fledgling pecked its immobilised limb.

Dad went in, and while we were shooing the cat again, a magpie flew down and took the glittering slide, new brother and all.

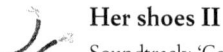

Her shoes II
Soundtrack: 'Cocktails for Two' performed by Spike Jones and his City Slickers

32A Wildwood Road

Viewed from under the table, a herd of legs mills below the chattering canopy of heads and clinking drinks. The men's pleated slacks are black or navy; their shoes standard black lace-ups, smelling of fresh Kiwi polish. They pursue peep toes, kitten heels, slingbacks, strappy white sandals with bows, mirror-shiny black patent leather. The women's stockinged legs are uniform American tan, except for one pair in seamed black fishnets sporting pointy red crocodile pumps, toes squeezed into a miniature cleavage, the heel a metal-tipped spike emitting crisp click-clacks on the parquet.

Later, the crowd gone, an angry exchange is overheard:

'Stilettos! How will we ever get rid of these frightful dents?'
'But darling, I couldn't very well order a woman to take off her shoes.'

Sugar and spice

Scole, Norfolk, England

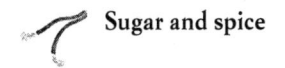

'Might as well turn the blighter into a curry, eh?' says Annie, my favourite aunt. Her voice is husky, her movements delicate despite her size.

'Right-oh,' says Livy. Dad's younger sister. Not as fat but much crabbier than Annie.

The two maiden aunts have released the duck from its hook in the pantry, and smacked it onto the square wooden table. I've been given a stool to stand on.

Within minutes, the air is filled with feathers, as the sisters' plump fingers pluck away colourful plumage. Using a slender knife, Annie slices meat and skin off the bones. Head, neck and innards have gone somewhere, but I don't want to think about that. I don't want to think about my uncles shooting wild birds yesterday. Dad says that's what they do in Norfolk.

A copper kettle is singing on top of the mammoth black Aga. Annie reaches for one of the stone jars crowded onto the side-shelf. She removes its stopper. An unfamiliar smell wafts across the kitchen table.

More ingredients appear – sultanas, rice, onions. Livy goes to fetch herbs from the garden. Hearing Grandima's tetchy call, Annie bustles out to the front parlour. I am on my own.

I pick up the jar and tip it towards me to see inside; it's filled to the brim with vivid ochre powder. I take a deep sniff. My nose flames and the jar smashes onto the black-and-white chequered flagstones.

At dinner my eyes are still sore. Viv asks why I'm crying.
Dad and his brothers are laughing. Uncle Frank launches into his stories about hunting tigers in India.

I never want to go there.

Item 8: Red Dragon, bamboo-and-ivory piece
from old Mrs Thonger's mah-jong set

I fear that my sisters are siding with my mother in disapproving of my wife.
I fear that my wife loved her dead poodle more than she ever loved me.
I fear that a lesser man might steal my wife.
I fear that my wife's mother talks about me and plots behind my back.

Sick day

32A Wildwood Road

My father's reading to me: Kipling's illustrated *Just So Stories*. Just us: Caro's at school, Mum's at work, Gerda's at college. His shiny head's wreathed in a blue smoke nest, delicate strands coiling upwards, splitting from the glowing tip of his cigarette.

Fog hovers over the ashtray on the bedside table. I've lined up his Camels packet and my inhaler, side by side like two dolls. He goes slowly so we can read my favourite line together: 'puffing up and puffing up into a great big lolloping humph'. His voice rumbles, mine wheezes out the words.

Our hands touch: I'm reaching for the inhaler; he's reaching for the packet.

Birthday
Soundtrack: 'Mackie Messer' sung by Hildegard Knef

32A Wildwood Road

My present from Mum and Dad is a lumpy parcel. I lift it off the breakfast table, suppressing my excitement. Will it be another animal to add to my collection?

'Be careful,' says Mum. Dad lights a cigarette. Viv is all eyes.

The parcel is heavy at one end, and it takes time to unpick the sticky-tape and striped wrapping paper. A large doll emerges, with a painted china head, nodding eyes, and stuck-on yellow hair. She is wearing shiny blue satin with a wide floppy lace collar.

Attached to her dress is a note in Mum's handwriting:
Hello Caroline, my name is Charlotte
You must love me

I sit her on my lap facing me to unpin the note. 'Oh, she's lovely,' I say, automatically.

Her head is so heavy that she lolls backwards. I catch her just in time and sit her back up.

Her eyes open with a click and stare at me.

The perfect dinner

32A Wildwood Road

Three artfully crafted crabs, thumbnail-sized: mother-of-pearl bodies, gold legs and pincers, a tiny ruby topping each eyestalk. Politely, the Thonger family members leaned forward to admire these jewelled confections bedded in tissue paper.

The hostess, Mrs Thonger, had opened the small parcel, a courtesy gift from the Ambassador's wife, while they sipped Dubonnets in the sitting room. They'd met once before, at the Embassy's drinks party welcoming Mr Thonger to his new job. Her stammered thanks revealed astonishment at her guest's generosity. She immediately pinned the three brooches onto her blouse to show her appreciation. A few minutes later, however, she had to take them off to put on her apron for dinner preparations. She ran upstairs to put the exquisite things away.

Once the first cork was pulled and canapés were circulating, the children were sent upstairs. In their mother's dressing-table drawer, tissue paper rustled.

'There's one each,' the younger girl whispered. 'We're just borrowing them.'

Back in the playroom, the crabs were guests of honour during that evening's playtime: terrorising the doll's house, stars of the puppet theatre. At the usual time, the children obeyed the call to get into pyjamas, go down for goodnights, go to bed. They made sure to put the crabs to bed, too.

When the men lit cigars and swirled cognac, Mrs Thonger led the way to the ladies' powder room, the flowers beside the washbasin still fresh, she noted with satisfaction. The evening had been a success; her husband's foot was now squarely on the Embassy ladder.

As the Ambassador's wife stood and turned to flush, a gleam at the bottom of the toilet bowl caught her eye: there nestled – minus several eyes and legs – the three gilded crabs.

Lair

32A Wildwood Road

The Olivetti clacks in staccato bursts behind the closed door downstairs. After several pings, it stops. Dad shouts my name and I lean over the banister.

'Is that silly girl there? Tell her I need a cup of tea.'

The door shuts and I go to find Gerda. She and Viv are reading the story about Paulinchen and her cautionary cats.

'Gerda, Daddy asked for some tea, please?'

'But Mr Songer likes not that I come into his special room, not for cleaning or nossing – ' says Gerda.

She closes the book. 'Come, you help me.'

We watch her make tea the English way.

'I'll take it in to Daddy.' Feeling brave, I take a breath and go in.

Thick velvet curtains keep out the daylight. A single lamp casts a ghostly pool of light over the desk. Crumpled paper spills out of the bin by Dad's feet. An eerie miasma hangs over his head; a worm of ash crawls down his waistcoat; countless stubs bristle beside the black typewriter.

I hurry forward to put the cup-and-saucer by his elbow. Sunk in reverie, he is oblivious. A sheet of paper lingers in the typewriter, blank except for two words: 'Your Majesty'.

Menace emanates from the walls; the room closes in. Toppling piles of yellowed newspapers encroach, lurch over the floor, slither across the ceiling. They will smother me in their smouldering embrace.

I back out of the door, breathless.

'Pooh,' says Gerda. 'You are schtinky.'

Item 9: 24-carat gold signet ring with the imprint of an owl on an oak branch – Thonger family crest

My mother and the Rokeby Venus

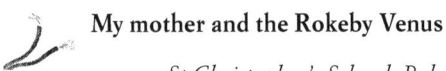

St Christopher's School, Belsize Lane, London NW3

A small group of us waited inside, almost an hour after the end of school. We kept an eye on the entrance gates, still open.

The other girls had to stay on because their fathers were picking them up after work. They asked why my mother was late too. 'Because she's been working,' I said.

Two other girls started quizzing me; their fathers were a doctor and an accountant. 'Is that the sort of work you're talking about? Don't you just mean doing housework?'

'No,' I said, 'she tells people about paintings.' Today was her first day at the National Gallery. She used to write essays after supper. She has piles of art books.

'What does she say about the paintings?' a small girl asked.

Invention was my forte. I cleared my throat and affected a plummy accent. 'Ladies and gentlemen, this is a loverly pitcher of a fraffly famous lady with no clothes on at all,' I said, waving curvaceous shapes into the air. Everyone fell about laughing.

The classroom door opened and we all turned our heads.

A woman walked in briskly: high heels, navy pencil skirt, waist-cinching jacket. Her gloves matched her pillbox hat with its jaunty veil. Her hair was tucked up neatly under it, and her lipstick glowed deep red.

My mother, I realised with a jolt: how dazzling, how smart, how put-together she was.

'Hurry up, we're going home,' she said, imperious.

All eyes were on her.

'Ooh, lookit 'er!' I blurted in cod Cockney. 'Wot a fancy titfer! Cor, ain't she done up posh!' I did an exaggerated version of her high-heeled, tight-skirted walk.

The others didn't laugh, and neither did she.

'Don't you dare speak to me like that,' she said. '*Ever.*' She turned away and clacked down the wooden stairs.

She didn't have to glance back – not once – to know I was following right behind.

A la carte

53 Park Lane, London W1

Dorchester Hotel
Sunday 1ˢᵗ September 1963

Festive Luncheon
Celebrating the 80ᵗʰ Birthday of
Friedrich Richard Vollmann

Pol Roger Brut Réserve   Château Latour 1950

~

Turtle Consommé with Sherry

~

Lobster Thermidor

~

Coquelet in Wine
Seasonal Vegetables

~

English Trifle

~

Port and Stilton

~

Coffee and Petits Fours served in the Lounge
H. Upmann Cuban Cigars from our Humidor

The Americans
Soundtrack: 'Frankie and Johnny' sung by Josh White

32A/32 Wildwood Road

'And these are our boys!' Kaye, the new neighbour, waved at the willow in her garden. A lanky sandy-haired youth unfolded from the tree, followed by a slighter, dark-haired version and a small blond boy my size. All three were lithe, muscular, tanned; they wore loose jeans and no tops. Slow, loping strides, arms hanging down, brilliant white teeth. Boys, but unlike any we knew. They stuck out their hands and shook everyone's across the fence, grinning with Sir's and Ma'am's, just like the cowboys in *Bonanza*. Dad didn't smile back. I sniggered: Caro was blushing, really blushing.

'You guys wanna come play in the bomb shelter?' Kevin slouched against the windowless concrete shed, unravelling some rope. Inside, it was damp and rank.

Filthy.

The boys sometimes left us in there at lunchtime – Kaye banged a pot to summon them, and they'd race indoors. Occasionally, Ian would hang back to loosen the knots, so they didn't chafe as much.

Filthy, bruised.

'*Schweinhund*,' we'd say, baring our teeth. Our accents were perfect. 'Shut up, Fritz,' he'd reply. That's how the game went.

Filthy, bruised, exhilarated.

We watched the boys sharpen torn-off twigs to make bows and arrows. With his first arrow, Kevin skewered a squirrel in one of our apple trees. 'See that?' he said to Caro, casually, only to her.

When Dad banned us from ever going over the fence again, or even talking to the boys, they took it better than we did. 'You were pretty good Nazis, for girls,' called Carl from the willow, and Ian flashed me the peace sign, as Dad hammered a higher section onto the old fence.

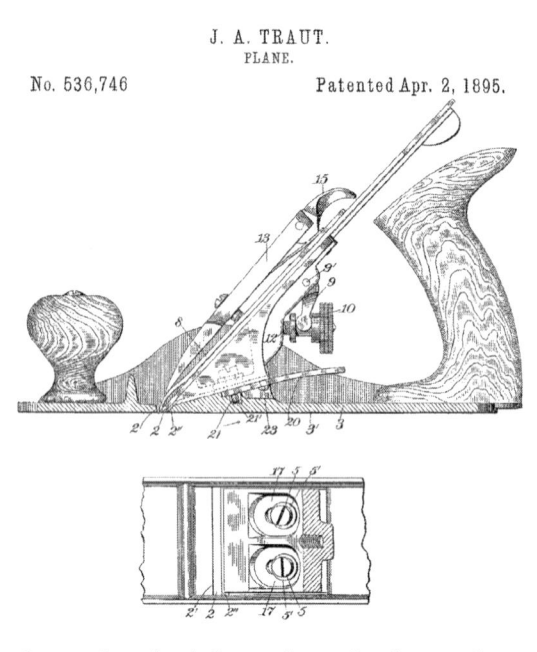

Item 10: Large hand plane, mahogany handle, worn, heavy

March 1964

Ehrang-Trier

Evie,

I have taken the decision not to get upset any more about Ursel, and I advise you to do the same. You cannot change a thing, so stop getting into such a state.

Malediction (part 1)

Font Romeu, Pyrénées-Orientales, France

One day during their summer holidays high up in the mountains, the mother makes a fuss about wanting to 'go for a little walk', just the two of them. Halfway up the local hillside, she comes to a stop and perches on a rock.

'Doesn't the Canigou look clear today?' she says, gazing into the distance.

'What are we doing here?' asks the girl, blinking in the bright sun. She sits down cross-legged on the arid grass, facing her mother. One hand caresses the cushion of tiny wildflowers beside her. A waft of wild thyme lifts into the warm air.

The mother pulls her skirt further down over her knees. She rummages in her shoulder bag.

'I wanted to talk to you,' she mumbles, almost too quiet to hear. A leaflet is pressed into the girl's hand. The cover says: *'What every girl needs to know, by Sister Maria, Convent of the Sacred Heart'*.

'You can read this on your own, Caroline,' says the mother, cheeks flushed. 'It will tell you all you need to know about The Curse.'

The girl nods in silence, fiddling with the leaflet. A grasshopper zips onto the shiny surface and pings off again into the juniper.

'Of course you know all about this, from other girls at school, don't you?' continues the mother. Without looking at her daughter she says, 'Good, then that's all sorted.'

They're walking back downhill; the girl's face is blank. She kicks up the dust under her sandals as her mind whirls. Why is her mother telling her to read something written by a nun about witchcraft? The only curses the girl is familiar with are in *Macbeth*. What would other girls know that she doesn't?

She sees her younger sister waving at the window and runs up the concrete stairs to the apartment. The leaflet is forgotten.

Bathroom secrets

Soundtrack: 'Black Bottom' performed by Bob Crosby and his orchestra

32A Wildwood Road

'We'll be in my room till tea's ready,' I said to Mum, as I ushered my three new schoolfriends up the stairs. It was the first time I'd been allowed to invite anybody to my house since starting senior school.

'Oh,' said Janie as I showed the three of them into my bedroom.
'Isn't your room big?' said Lydia.
'Where are the rest of your dolls?' asked Stephanie.
'I know what,' I said, filled with sudden inspiration. 'Come and look in here.' And I led the trio across the landing into the family bathroom.

'What's that?' asked Lydia, her eyes fixed on the porcelain item between the wash basin and the bath-tub. The other two girls followed her gaze.
'It's a bidet,' I said proudly. 'Mum's just had it fitted.'
'A bee-day?' mimicked Stephanie.
'Yes, it's French I think,' I said.
'But what's it for?' asked Lydia. 'Washing your feet?'

'I'll show you,' I said with a giggle, bending down to turn on the tap. A fountain of water shot up towards the ceiling. 'We can all do it,' I said, 'but we have to take off our knickers.'

The three girls gawked at me, speechless.

Without a qualm, I slipped off my brown school knickers, hitched up the pleated tweed school skirt, and sat down on the fountain. An involuntary shriek bounced around the bathroom.

'My go, me, me, me,' the three of them clamoured, pushing to be first. Four pairs of brown knickers lay scattered on the floor. Soon the air was filled with squeals of delight.

The door burst open. Mum. She almost slipped over on the wet floor.
'How dare you, Caroline?' she yelled. 'Stop that at once!'

Tea was a silent affair.

Item 11: Bidet, white porcelain

The doctor

1 Upper Wimpole Street, London W1

'All done, young lady. Here you are, for the new pills,' says Dr Ratner, scribbling at his desk, and Mum's helping me on with my duffel coat and fumbling to open her handbag for the prescription. She hasn't even had time to take off her gloves.

'See you in six weeks, chum,' he says, sweeping the door open, his ginger-and-white reflection in the ornate hallway mirror bowing us out.

The receptionist carefully closes the door behind us, and we're out into the genteel Marylebone traffic. I try not to step on cracks; I'm getting used to my new, stronger glasses and perspective is still warped. After a few steps, Mum adjusts her brisk walking pace for me; she holds out her hand and I hang onto it with both of mine. A taxi with its light on passes slowly, but she doesn't hail it. She stops by a row of railings and crouches, perching on her heels in front of me, skirt taut over her knees. She holds my arms through the coat and takes a breath.

'I like Dr Ratner, he's funny,' I say before she can begin. 'His hair sticks up like a broom.'
'Darling, it's very, very important that you don't tell your father where we've been. Promise me?' she says. Of course I won't tell. I know about secrets; I have lots. My buttock feels hot where the injection went in.
'Can I tell Caro?'
'Try not to, darling. We'll say I took you to Mr Lockwood's. You had a sore tooth.'

Orange

Soundtrack: 'The Gas-Man Cometh' by Flanders and Swann

32A Wildwood Road

Middle of the night; I'm sitting bolt-upright in bed, quivering. Black shadows flutter across my curtains; the room glows orange from the street-lamps.

Footsteps come running down the corridor. A voice shouts, *'Feuer! Feuer!'* Doors bang; Gerda bursts into my room. Pungent smoke swirls in with her.

She tugs me off the bed.

'No, I don't want to!' I pull against her. My nose and eyes are stinging; I can't catch my breath.

I'm hauled onto the landing. Viv's coughing nearby; somebody is urging us downstairs. Yellow-and-orange smog funnels up the stairwell. It's too dense to get through.

'Get in here!' comes Mum's muffled voice, as we're shoved back up upstairs and into her bedroom.
'Jam these wet towels under the door,' shouts Dad. 'Do *not* open the windows.' He thumps his way back downstairs again.

Taps running, bucketfuls of water sloshing, continuous coughing. Something monstrous rumbles and crackles. I imagine flames licking through the floor from below, devouring my feet.

'Where's the fire brigade? They should be here by now.' Mum is by the window, peering down the road.

Viv has crawled under the blankets. Gerda starts singing German nursery rhymes, but chokes on the words. We're holding cotton hankies from Mum's dressing table over our mouths and noses.

Breathing hurts.

All the house lights go out and there's only the orange glow outside.
'Is the house going to burn down?' My voice is a croak; no one replies.

A blue light races across the ceiling, over and over. I jump to the window. Down below, men in boots and helmets advance towards our house. Some have torches, others have axes.

There's a rush of noise and shouting; then we're outside, barefoot in the dark, blankets over our nightclothes. A figure staggers from the smoke, retching and sputtering, face black.

Dad.

We're offered shelter next door; their lounge carpet is rough and none of us can sleep. When cold morning light seeps in, we tiptoe out and across the driveway to our house.

The front lawn is peppered with black smuts. Still smouldering, the sofa sags upside-down, its springs sticking out. A burnt-vegetable stench of blackened kapok fills the air. Nearby sprawls the exploded black-and-white TV set, its twisted innards exposed.

'What's happened to the goldfish?' asks Viv. I shiver in my pyjamas.

The front door gapes open. The adults go in.

Radical

Marylebone Clinic, 144 Harley Street, London W1

'Well, Podge, Shrimp . . . Well – your mother's having an operation.' Dad sat at breakfast, rubbing his hands as if they were cold. Mum folded and refolded her napkin.

I could tell it was something bad.

She's lying in a metal-framed hospital bed. Her face is ashy-white. She tries to smile.

I want to hold her hand, but when I move closer I realise there are tubes sprouting out of it. And not only there: she has tubes coming from under the blanket, and more tubes stuck into her neck.

Viv tugs my sleeve.

Yellow liquid is moving through one of the tubes, down into a container under the bed.

Dad sits, jogging the bed. He shushes us, doesn't even let us say hello. He takes a sheaf of papers from the inside pocket of his jacket.

'Good, good, you're looking much better,' he says. The only reply is a groan.
Dad spreads out the papers onto the bed.
'If you could just sign here and here,' he says to her. 'Then that's all the tax forms sorted.'

I feel queasy. Under the floral nightdress, one side of her chest is flatter than the other.

The yellow liquid moves again, down into the container under the bed.

May 1965

The White House, Albany Street, London NW1

Dickie,

So you are not coming to London. I perfectly understand your reason for doing what you did. She will just have to manage without you.

I fear that there's whispered conniving, that my wife is being misguided.
I fear the scythe-eyed demons sitting atop the gateposts – they mean us harm.
I fear for the Royal Family because, through our Jane Grey connection, I am the weak link.
I fear there is a plot to remove me.
I fear that my letters have been misinterpreted by inferior intellects.
I fear that I am to be thrown to the wolves.

PART TWO

Taken
Soundtrack: 'I Hold Your Hand In Mine' by Tom Lehrer

53 Hillway, London N6

'Mum, where are we going?'
'You've gone the wrong way!'
We call out at the same moment.

Veering from the usual route into Highgate Village, she drives us through unfamiliar white gates, then slowly down a long steep hill. Below us, London stretches away in a haze: the Post Office Tower, a glint of the river.

'We'll be late,' says Viv, craning forwards.
'We were going to take the bus,' I say.

The road is lined with boxy black-and-white houses. Outside a house like all the others, we come to an abrupt stop. The flowerbeds are straggly.

Mum clears her throat. 'Get out, girls,' she says. 'You're not going to school today.'

We stand uncertainly beside the Mini. Mum takes a key out of her handbag. Ducking under a creeper twining from an upstairs balcony, she leads us to the front door. It jams. With a couple of shoves, she gets it open.

Despite the summer weather, the house is cold and dim inside. No furniture, bare floorboards. Mum ushers us through the hallway towards the back, and opens a squeaky garden door. We're standing on a cramped terrace of uneven paving slabs; there's an overgrown pond, some grass.

With her back to the patio wall she clears her throat several times, then speaks. 'So, this is our new home. The three of us.' She clutches my arm and hugs me awkwardly. I reach my free hand out to Viv.

Back indoors, we look into more blank rooms. My thoughts go back to getting dressed this morning, finding my wardrobe emptied, not saying anything because Mum was in a rush. Our clothes must be in the Mini's boot.

While Mum is running water down in the kitchen, I beckon Viv to sit with me at the top of the stairs.
'It's creepy here,' I whisper. 'As if we've been kidnapped.'
'And we're missing the last day of term!' she whispers back.

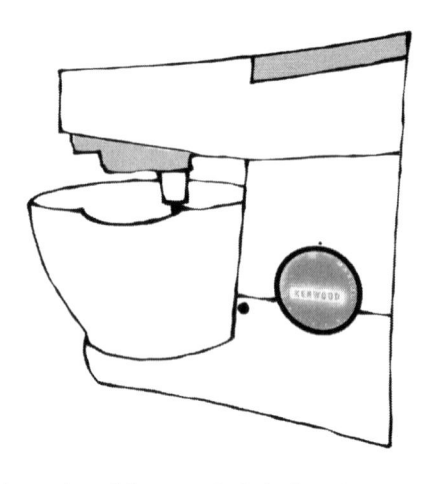

Item 12: (On order) A701A model Kenwood Chef, white/duck-egg blue, opaque glass bowl, K-beater, dough hook, whisk, liquidiser

Taken again

Grand Hotel, Eastbourne, Sussex

'But *darlings*, I had no idea where you'd gone, no idea how to find you!'

Dad's volley is directed at both of us, but as I'm sitting in the front seat of the Austin Cambridge and Viv's in the back, it's me he's gripped by the shoulders. His face is close; spit flecks me as he talks.

'She left a note on the coffee table in the sitting room. A note! Can you imagine how I felt?' He ends with a whimper, as if he might cry.

We're parked outside the seaside hotel we've been staying in all week. Mum's mostly been ignoring us, even though we're supposed to be on holiday.

Dad drives us to a village. After a slow walk along the shore, with Viv getting her shoes wet in the scummy surf, we sit down at a beachside café.

'What's Mummy been saying about me?'

I don't know what to answer. Viv's gurning at the back of a spoon. 'She said we should see you, Daddy,' I say.

It's the wrong thing.

'But Callet, *she's* only talking through legal people,' he says, jabbing his finger at me. His voice is high and whiny. I'm glad there's nobody else in the café. 'I was forced to wait until my *lawyer* told me where you were.'

When we've finished our fizzy drinks, he drives us back to the hotel. Mum's at the front entrance. She doesn't speak to him when he calls to her out of the car window.

'Did your father say anything about me?' she asks, back in the gloomy lounge.

Item 13: Scrimshawed walrus-tusk letter opener
in the form of a fish, probably Inuit

Rock-Ola

Grand Hotel Eastbourne

On day one, the receptionist warns the two of us that the staircase to '>>>The Ballroom' is out of bounds. When she isn't watching, we creep down through heavy doors, our footsteps dust-muffled, into a cavernous, dim space, sheets covering piled chairs. Looming in the darkness, a jukebox.

Mum spends hours at the back of the hotel's fusty lounge, on the phone to her 'slister'. We're mystified: we have no aunts on her side. She puts her hand over the receiver and glares if we try to listen in.

Armed with coins sneaked from her purse, we plug in the jukebox. We press a button labelled 'C&W'. Syrupy guitars and twangy voices wash over us: we snigger. No one comes to stop us. We practise our American accents and play table tennis in semi-darkness – we've found a folding table, balls, bats. Neither of us thinks of trying the light switches.

Tammy Wynette is on repeat-play; her voice cracks with overblown emotion and we yell along, mimicking her stretched syllables: 'Dee – eye – vee – oh – arr – see – ee', acting out every phrase: her pitiful little boy! The tears dripping down her cheek! And the highlight, that bit about 'custardy' being a hurting word: we mime custard fights and die laughing.

When we're out of money and go back up, Mum's packing. We're leaving. Words we can already spell begin to take on meaning.

July 1966
Letter from Eastbourne
(translated from German)

My dear old Pop,

So, yesterday morning I left Wildwood Road for good. There's still a battle ahead until I can rid myself of Richard - but the worst of it, all that agonised soul-searching, is finally over and done with. You'll be relieved to know that I actually listened to you, and I admit that in the end I did what you advised. Now you and I can get back to normal again!

The children do not have a single word of sympathy for their father. When I asked them if they'd prefer me to make up with him, they replied without a moment's thought, 'No, people who are not happily married don't belong together.' Heartless or plain common sense?

Because it was all so last-minute, we're in Eastbourne's most expensive hotel. It's full of ancient old people with arthritis and mink capes. The Mini's parked in a sea of Rollses and Jags.

The children are enchanted by the new house. I showed them around yesterday, before we drove down to the south coast.

Don't forget that you mustn't tell anyone where we are at the moment, or what we're doing.

So now I'll bid you goodnight from my grandiose surroundings, to get some shut-eye beside those snoring girls.

Sending you a loving kiss, your Ursel.

PART THREE

53 Hillway, Highgate, London N6

September 1966

Charming detached house in mock-Tudor style, featuring bow-fronted window and east-facing balcony. The downstairs area comprises hallway, 2 reception rooms, cloakroom, kitchen, and door to back garden. Upstairs are the master bedroom and 3 smaller bedrooms, the bathroom, plus an airing cupboard. All bedrooms have wash basins. Oil-fired central heating, oil tank at rear. Garage for one car.

The property is conveniently situated halfway down the hill within easy walking distance to the Heath and Parliament Hill. Highgate Village can be accessed through Waterlow Park. There are local shops in Swains Lane below Holly Lodge Estate, as well as the 214 bus stop to nearby Kentish Town underground station.

Asking price: £14,000

Item 14: A stick of French sealing wax, red, partly melted

Malediction (part 2)

53 Hillway

The young teenager is getting undressed for bed. There's a dark-brown stain in her knickers. She has no idea what it is, but filled with a nameless shame she rams the pants into her bottom drawer. She can't tell anyone, not even her sister. Sometime later the mother uncovers her secret. She seems more sad than angry.

'*Ach, natürlich*,' she says. 'We women, we all have to deal with The Curse.'

The following month the pain is sudden, unexpected and agonising. And the next month. The girl still doesn't understand what it is, believing her mother has cursed her.

If only she'd read the leaflet.

Hands

Titisee, Baden-Württemberg, West Germany

A summer holiday in Germany. The girl hunches on her chair in the crowded guesthouse restaurant, thin arms braced, each exhalation a loud wheeze that draws an irritated tut from her mother. Her stomach hurts, a constant burning. Her sister's knife slices into a juicy schnitzel. It smells delicious.

'Das Kind darf keine Soße!' Her grandmother's ringed hand hovers over the girl's plate, deflecting the waiter's gravy-boat: no cream sauce with tiny mushrooms, nor melted butter speckled with parsley. Whatever it is, she's not allowed it.

Yesterday, her mother and the village doctor talked over the girl's head; he prodded her distended stomach, laughing as she flinched. She'd overeaten, he said, ignoring her thinness. He didn't ask about the daily pills that make her hands shake.

'You love our wonderful Bavarian food, naturally. But now you diet. No more ice cream!'

Her mother passes her a flaccid lemon slice – to make it nicer, she says. The girl takes a mouthful of boiled potato and reverts to her hunched position.

Her sister inclines her head towards the next table: six adults wreathed in cigar smoke emit a mass sigh as the waitress sets down six Knickerbocker Glories. She hopes they get stomach pains too. Her sister stifles a laugh.

The table cleared, her sister takes her elbow. They stand and walk out together, heads up.

Outside, the girl is soon left hanging on her grandmother's arm, as if she were the old woman. Spots bloom in front of her eyes; she stoops and coughs to clear the phlegm filling her lungs. Her grandmother's face creases in distaste.

She's interrupted by a teasing voice.

'C'mon, slowcoach.' Her sister's beside her and takes both her hands, tugging her upright and two steps further, before skipping ahead to catch up with their mother.

Paean

Titisee

How
charming
these tree-laden hills
gushes the brochure pure healthy air
mother and grandmother repeat the mantra along
a mesh of bleak grey autobahns
our arrival under tarnished pewter clouds
puddled carpark awash entrance cloaked in gloom
fir trees louring hearing our moans Mum's angry face spits
we're going to have a lovely holiday between clenched teeth of
persistent drizzle
the forbidding forest looms phantasms haunt my dreams eidolons
hobgoblins spectres wraiths
on our cheerless walks I crack
the conundrum the rain must have unleashed
ancient denizens primeval pranksters lure visitors then pounce
with flabby batter fat and gristle suffocating flour-sauce white-out
thick sickly crème wallpaper paste all the food a fraud
Schwarzwälderkirschtorte
unpronounceable mouthful of sweet nothing
sterile sponge insipid bottled gobs shaving-foam froth
faux fake-cake sogged cardboard base unwholesome hoax
sickening my sister
ersatz chocolate
disenchantment

Typical

53 Hillway

After breakfast, the two women gossip about Ursula's colleagues – all women, English-German interpreters like her. Elsie H: a harsh accent – so snobby, she despises anyone who'd converted. Eva W: a gentle soul but she only talks about her relatives – all that fuss over her daughters. Elsa B: a grand lady, but can you believe her husband has to run the bath for her? She can't do a thing for herself! And her appalling English!

Oma says, '*Na so was, gräßlich!*' and shakes with laughter.
Their heads sway together.
Ursula's braying; she rubs tears out of her eyes and adds, 'So *dreadfully* Jewish!'

Item 15: Coat-hanger, padded, floral pattern,
used to discipline teenage girls

Slow burn

Godalming, Surrey, England

One of Dad's Sundays. We're invited to lunch with Frank and Maureen.

Dad's youngest brother is dark and stocky. And blustering. His military moustache tickles when he kisses us. His wife – Maureen – is fair. More reserved, calm even. She's a newish aunt and we're still intrigued by her Scots brogue. Later – when we're alone – Viv will mimic the same brogue. I'll fall down laughing.

It's already past midday so the two of us are hoping lunch will be soon. Frank has plans for the barbecue out on their patio. Our glasses of orange squash accompany Maureen's small sherry. We help her make salad, and gather plates and cutlery. The two brothers, whisky-and-sodas in hand, do battle with the contraption outside.

Their voices carry through the kitchen door's reeded glass; we can't help eavesdropping as the coals continue to refuse to ignite and the meat sits raw on the side.

'What d'you mean, my fault?' shouts Frank.

'It bloody well was,' retorts Dad. 'What about that shirt of mine you borrowed in 1942?'

Maureen titters nervously; we smile back. She seems less used to this kind of thing than we are.

Dad charges indoors. 'Right, we're leaving!' He bundles us into the car. As he revs the engine, we wave unconvincingly to Maureen. Frank has disappeared. A pathetic plume of smoke rises from the patio.

On the return journey the car skids along the narrow Surrey lanes. We're over the speed limit the whole way. At one point, Dad drives straight across a roundabout. About an hour later we've arrived white-faced at our front door. Our mother's expression is puzzled – we're early.

Before she can ask 'Did you have a nice time?' Dad has driven away.

'Uncle Frank has a new barbecue,' we say, as we step inside, stamping to disguise our trembling legs.

Family fixture

53 Hillway

knobbly-kneed hagbag bandy
scrawny chicken legs clunky-hipped
gait of a pantomime dame bustling
busybody graspy hands flap
on arms too much crook and sinew
dark moles sprout hairs on sour
wrinkled cheeks faded brown
monkey eyes meagre lashes drawn-on
brows tan forehead like waxed leather
dulled straw hair side-parted pinned
with a single kirby grip a parody of gauche
girlishness grim-faced merriment lines fan
from thin strips of lips loose and livid
pegs of worn teeth a tongue too pink too tart
she thinks she's being English what
a joke with that hokey Plinter accent

Charmed

Route Limoges – Cahors, south-western France

We're driving across France in summer, destination: the Pyrenees. I'm in front, navigating. Viv's jammed into the back seat with camping gear and roadside purchases. At least she has peaches and her special pillow.

Avoiding the *autoroutes* and their *péages*, Dad drives our entire three-day journey on narrow D-roads. The further south, the dustier and more potholed the roads. The car speeds along.

He doesn't shave, and his black beard is woven with ginger-and-grey. Overnighting at campsites, we get looks from the large French families in tents around us. I overhear the word *'enlèvement'* and feel like I'm constantly blushing.

Early on the third morning it's already hot, the parched fields chirruping with crickets. We pass isolated, red-roofed farm-houses and few cars. Poplar shadows flicker past hypnotically.

A flurry of brown feathers; a violent double-bump sensation under the car. I daren't look behind. Dad doesn't slow down but I see him squint at the rear-view mirror several times. After a while he starts muttering, banging the steering wheel:
us or the chicken
I couldn't help it darlings
too dangerous to brake
us or the chicken
us or the chicken
We drive on, faster. Hot dampness under my arms. Partially obscured by overhanging branches, a large inverted triangle crosses my peripheral vision. The red lettering is unmistakable: STOP.

There's no let-up on the accelerator. Blurry black fills the windscreen, roars.

We're lurching up, across and down the other side, my stomach flip-flopping as if on a roller-coaster. Broken white lines glittering; horns blasting; machines fracturing around us. Cars and trucks and caravans whizz by in both directions.

Nothing but buzzing insects. Dad hasn't flinched and the car hasn't stopped. My sister's gripping the empty fruit crate on her lap; squashed peaches surround her. Our hearts must be racing in unison.

I look down at the Michelin map.

It's the N-89, a three-lane *route nationale*.

The chicken or us.

Weight

Lac des Bouillouses, Pyrénées-Orientales, France

A grunt makes me turn. Buckles scrape against stone. It's Dad. Over he goes.

He seems surprised to be tipping backwards. His legs whisk up. I note the patterned tread on his soles as he slides away, accelerating down the shining rock face.

We'd been traversing the steep side of the lake, zigzagging up a disused fishermen's track that skirted rock walls and vanished into sodden clumps of grass.

Caro and I were grumbling behind him, 'I'm soaked, I'm tired, why are we the only people on this side?'

He overheard and put on his threatening grin, saying, '*Darlings,* today's adventure brings us *this* way.' He took more things out of my rucksack until I was carrying a single water bottle. His pack was so overloaded that it dwarfed him.

'But I'm strong,' I said.
'You're an eleven-year-old shrimp,' he said, 'your sister can help.'
'I'm only thirteen,' she said, 'and my rucksack's heavy,' but he didn't hear and sent us ahead.

He hangs spreadeagled in the air before hitting the boulders far below, bouncing, a faraway doll somersaulting headlong into the lake. A dozen ducks fly up. Ripples fan out from the foaming spot where he went in.

Screams stick in my throat as Caro drops her pack and leaps down the rocks, finding invisible footholds. She reaches the lake and wades in, drags him into sitting position. He leans sideways. She's shaking his arm.

Her voice carries: 'Dad, your head.' He is wearing something red and flowing, a long red veil covering his face and white t-shirt.

She looks up, at me.

The great outdoors

Lac des Bouillouses

Up to his neck in water, Dad is spluttering and struggling to sit up. One arm clutches a sleeping bag billowing on the frothing, rain-pitted surface. His face is lead-grey, his breath comes in shallow gasps. Blood wells purple from the gash on his head.

Wading in, I wrench at the sleeping bag; my fingers are numb. I tear at its dead weight again and again, sitting in the icy water, reeling him in, slowly, painfully. Viv is up top, looking down.

There's a fisherman in the shallows beside me. He's run barefoot from the opposite side of the lake, across the dam and along the shore. He helps me get Dad up, one on each arm; we're all drenched. *'Monsieur, monsieur,'* he's saying, alarmed. 'Your head. You need a doctor.'

Dad is shouting at him in perfect French, telling him to go away, to mind his own damned business, that *tout va bien*.

'Et vous, Madame, vous êtes sûre?' he says to me. I gaze at our rescuer helplessly, and nod my head.

Hands up, he reluctantly turns away.

Madame. He thinks I'm an adult.

Just desserts

53 Hillway

Mum and Oma at the kitchen table. Mum holds a flimsy blue airmail letter: her cousin Dodo's distinctive arty writing. 'Nice, France' postmarked on the back. She slits it carefully open.

Mum says, 'Well I never. She simply fell forward into her pudding.'

Oma says, 'Who fell where? Did you say Dodo fell?'

Mum says, 'Daisy. Tante Daisy. She fell into the pudding, quite dead. What a lovely way to go.'

Oma's brow puckers.

Oma says, 'My sister? Into the pudding? And in front of her poor daughters? How very inconsiderate.'

A clink of silver on porcelain.

Mum says, 'Well, she was 80, you know. Will you be flying to Nice for the funeral?'

Another clink.

Oma says, 'Quite possibly, I suppose. One must observe the niceties. But that's so typical of Daisy – only ever thinking about herself.'

With her cake fork, Oma scoops up the last yellow crumb on her plate. She brings it carefully to her lips.

Item 16: Baked Jewish cheesecake: eggs, butter, full-fat cream cheese, sugar, lemon rind, a little flour, handful sultanas, lined with crushed digestive biscuits

Years passed, and the front door still stuck

53 Hillway

Summertime homework: in bikinis, on blankets on the grass, munching fragrant apples off the tree. And Mickey – Caro's kitten – nestled close. When he grew up, he wouldn't snuggle up, but deigned to sunbathe nearby, in the rockery.

The balcony outside my room, purple-perfumed, wisteria-wrapped – a place I'd sometimes hide and cry. But also: the giant pink bath where we could both lie submerged, entwined, mermaid-haired. When Caro started her period, I'd sit on the matching pink toilet so we could still chat.

My roaming hamsters gnawing at Mum's groovy new Scandinavian furniture. She swore at them, brandishing her small glass of neat Punt e Mes, and we sang, raucously, along with the stereo: *Reach Out I'll Be There*, *Silence is Golden*, *A Saucerful of Secrets*.

We drank in visitors: lodgers, family, colleagues. Every suppertime, the house, our sanctuary, opened its arms.

And one day, inevitably, Dad turned up.

The Highgate Tearooms

Soundtrack: 'Phonetic Punctuation' by Victor Borge

50 Highgate High Street, London N6

One Sunday, after Matins at St Michael's, Dad invited us for elevenses, and for once we agreed to join him.

The place hummed with chatty, churchy people. Dad was in good spirits; we piled jam on our scones and traded funny accents. He hooted when we mimicked our teachers – Madame Millar's Frenchy English, Miss Saunders' strangled vowels: '... *airnd* the greatest of these is *Chair-ra-tay*'.

I took on the vicar's pious drone. 'Let us spare a thought for those afflicted by famine.' Spot on. I squinted over my glasses. 'And dearly beloved, we already know what *special* words of *comfort* dear old Jesus *Christ* would have for the *starving* people of Biafra.' I waited for Dad's guffaw.

Silence. He was staring at his plate.

'It's so utterly boring, the sermon.' Seconds ticked by. 'The same old – '

The tea-set leaped as his fist hammered down on the table; we jumped in our seats. His chair squealed and he partly stood up, throwing a shadow over the white cloth.

'Never say that, Vivvy, never!' he thundered, his voice drowning out every other. 'It will do you no good!' His wonky eye bulged; his good eye narrowed. My appetite vanished.

Heads turned – big men shouting wasn't on the menu.

'No. Good. In the end.' He pursed his lips and sat back.

Something rose up in me, and it wasn't an apology.

Nosy

Channing School for Girls, The Bank, London N6

I'm not one of the Posse. After a cursory interrogation in the school toilets – mainly about my mother's face – I'm baffled about why they'd even bothered. I'd quickly been rated unqualified to join their ranks.

Noses are the Posse's obsession: all the girls spend long minutes in front of the common-room mirror. Most non-Posse girls are too wrapped up in their private hells concerning burgeoning body hair, periods, breasts or lack of, how to put on makeup and above all, how to meet boys, to worry unduly about noses. I'm surprised, sitting on my own at lunch, as three Posse members sit down around me. I stop eating.

Sarah begins. 'Your nose is a lovely shape, isn't it, Viv? Just right. If any of us had a nose job, we'd ask the surgeon to do one just like yours. Wouldn't we?' The other two nod, unsmiling.

'It's perfect,' they say in unison. I wait.

Franky leans across the table and segues smoothly, her voice low. 'So, actually we've got things to ask you. About sex. Intercourse.'

I feel used. And delighted. I've been noticed.

A passion so confused

Channing School

Miss Macrae has been directing from the back of the classroom, a tweedy hulk looming in the half-shadows. She always makes us act out Shakespeare; we've cleared a space at the front.

It's the casket scene from *The Merchant of Venice*, with Dawn and Alison as Bassanio and Portia. They make a handsome couple. Alison: those blue eyes, blonde ponytail, high cheekbones. Dawn: sassy, self-aware, dark-eyed.

Turn you where your lady is
And claim her with a loving kiss.

Their lips almost touch. For a few seconds, we are entranced.

From the back of the room, a wave of smirking giggles erupts as a sheet of paper is passed around: Lesley's latest cartoon.

Riotous laughter blots out the performers.

'Oh, for bloody hell's sake!' Macrae's roar fills the room. A missile hurtles across our heads, and falls into the far corner. The blackboard rubber. '*So* immature – your puny little minds will *never* appreciate the world of fine literature, or art, or beauty.'

She hasn't spotted the cartoon that now reaches the last desk, mine. It's a viciously accurate caricature of our English teacher: whopping breasts, caterpillar eyebrows, stick legs. In tiny writing, the title: *Miss McLesbo*. A squeamish sensation passes through me; I fold the paper and hide it under my jumper.

Macrae marches to the front of the class, gesturing brusquely for Dawn and Alison to sit down. Her eyes sear the female collective. She still doesn't know.

'You will spend the next twenty minutes learning Portia's speech until you're word-perfect: "The quality of mercy is not strained". No talking. Or you'll all be staying behind for detention.'

I start murmuring the lines: learning by heart is easy. Dad's always reciting at us. I'll be in Miss Macrae's good books again in no time.

'All You Need Is Love' is going around in my head.

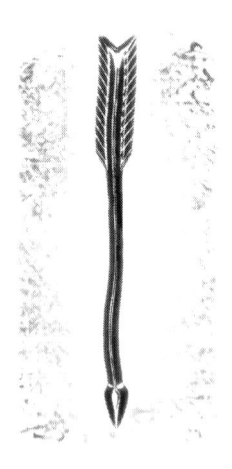

Item 17: Parker fountain pen with refillable reservoir
(hand-me-down); blue-black school ink

Way ahead of me

53 Hillway

It was my first date and not even real – I was a stopgap: my sister ordered me to be Lydia's replacement on a double date at the Golders Green Odeon. We were going to see *Little Big Man*. I was dizzy with the honour of being invited, and with the hope that I'd learn something, anything, about sex. Or kissing. Or teenage boys.

I agonised over what to wear, not wanting to lure Lydia's boyfriend and break the rules, but not wanting to seem uptight. Caro always wore a thin top and miniskirt when they went out; I was repulsed by the idea of making myself accessible to groping hands. I wore my scarlet belted trench coat over black T-shirt and trousers.

When the doorbell rang, my heart started hammering. I tried to act nonchalant on my way downstairs. The two boys gave me a glance and then continued chatting with Caro. I nipped into the kitchen to say goodbye to Mum and show her my outfit. I struck some poses.

She put her hands on her hips and didn't smile. 'It's a good thing you're not good-looking,' she said, 'because you're a prick-teaser.'

'What?' I'd heard the word, had no idea what it meant but knew the tone. I laughed.

'I said, you're a prick-teaser, that's what you are.' She was both smiling and angry now.

'Yes, aren't I?' was all I could think of. Out of my depth, flailing.

Walking out, catching a glimpse in the hallway mirror, I buttoned the coat up to my neck and it stayed that way all evening. Twenty seconds of Lydia's boyfriend's pursed, prudish, pimply mouth on mine was all the kissing practice I got.

The boyfriend's verdict, later, via Caro, via Lydia: your sister's nice but not sexy. At all.

*I fear my daughters may not want to visit because they have a new kitten at their mother's.
I fear that my younger daughter might tell my ex-wife that she and I were forced to share a double bed at the Aldeburgh B&B.
I fear that the money I borrowed from my elder daughter's bank account may never be returned to her.*

Jeremiad
Soundtrack: 'Aquarius' sung by the original cast of Hair

Flat 2 Southwood Hall, Muswell Hill Road, London N6

The usual boredom. Saturday: trying to stop Dad buying too much at the butcher's and greengrocer's; walking back laden with bags, through cold, wet Highgate Woods. Sunday: shunting all his tea-chests from one room to the other, as if the flat would ever stop being a dump. Let's shift some of this gubbins, Dad says every time. My hands always end up with splinters; dust flies about and Viv has to use her puffer. Two hours to make boeuf bourguignon – a good old proper Sunday lunch, Dad's mantra – one of three recipes he knows out of *Mastering the Art of French Cooking*, the others being chicken chasseur and beef stroganoff. I'm sick of them all. There's enough for six and he eats most of it. Then yawning and stretching he says, Your old man might need a bit of a zizz and he slopes off into his bedroom. I say, softly, Back to the Woods? and Viv gives the thumbs-up, but as soon as I turn the latch there's a heavy hand on my shoulder and Dad in my ear, You're going without me, Callet? Without your father? And Viv says, We thought you were asleep, but his eyes are drilling into mine, he's squeezing my shoulder and says, Darling – can't you just wait? He slams the front door, and now he's propelling me back into the kitchen. Passing the long mirror, he spots my reflection, which gives it all away: eyes rolling, shoulders shrugged. So what, I'm a teenager. I back against the sink, he towers over me and Viv slumps at the far end of the table. What if complete strangers invited you to China, Callet? he begins, and what if these lovely people gave you their own warm clothes and boots and guided you up this special mountain? He scratches his beard, a repulsive rasping. And what if they risked their lives to help you all the way to the top, where you were surrounded by the world's most beautiful scenery? I say nothing. What if – after those lovely people had spent a fortune and sacrificed so much for you – what if you had nothing to say, Callet, and the only thing you did was shrug your shoulders?

We're Wards of Court, shouts the Voice in my Head. *You can't tell us what to do.*

And stop calling me that.

Signature

53 Hillway

Mirabel, Mum's goddaughter, asked straight out why Mum had divorced Richard. The four of us, without Caro, were at the kitchen table.

'He was terribly unfair to Caroline,' said Mum, handing out platefuls of crispy spaghetti bake.

'Salad?' said Oma, wielding oversized wooden servers.

'But darling Uzi, he was always so jolly with Sebby and me. He adored his girls. I can't believe he meant it.' Mirabel's eyes were rimmed with black liner and she'd plucked her brows into arches, complementing the exaggerated Oxford slur she affected since starting university.

'Well, I suppose so. It was either him or me, really,' said Mum.

'There you are,' said Oma, and dabbed her mouth with her napkin. The topic was apparently dealt with.

After dinner, I put out the Dresden coffee set and leaned on the counter, waiting for the kettle to boil. The other three chatted about Oxford and Mirabel's new stepmother.

I picked up Mum's faded brown wallet: the familiar smell of leather and perfume. I took out her driving licence to admire her former pompadour hairstyle and sloping signature. Another thickness of card revealed older licences; I leafed through them. The last one was signed with a different name. Greyer, faded ink. Double-check: definitely her writing. It felt illicit. I pushed everything back and closed the wallet.

'Who's RU Harman?' I heard myself asking, interrupting.

'It's Ursula,' said Mirabel.

A click from the kettle.

'What?'

'Didn't you know? She was married before.' Her head bobbed from side to side, from me to my mother.

'No she wasn't.'

Mum's voice was calm, her tone unfamiliar. 'Ted was my first husband.'

'How's that coffee coming along?' said Oma.

Apprentissage

Waterlow Park, Highgate Hill, London N6

'Let's go down to the Dell,' murmurs Jill. 'Nobody's looking.'

Surrounded by leafy bushes and thickets of reeds, our Dell is the perfect hiding place from the all-day tennis tournament in the park opposite school. For a while the five of us exult in our shared lack of sporty prowess, chattering and sunbathing, while the grass tickles our bare legs and the sky soars blue above our heads.

'Shame we haven't got the Ouija board,' says somebody. Lydia sits up.
'Shall we play the She-game, see if it's successful this time?'
'I'll be It,' says Jill. 'If it works for me, then we'll know it's real.'
'And I'll be Cantor,' says Lydia.

Jill lies on her back, arms folded across her peppermint-striped school dress, eyes closed. She looks relaxed. The other four of us kneel beside her, two on each side. Lydia looks at each of us, face serious. When she's sure we are all paying attention, she starts the ritual, each utterance repeated four times.

'She looks pale.'
'She looks ill.'
'She *is* ill.'
'She is *very* ill.'
'She is dying.'
And then, *sotto voce*, twice around the group, in the same monotone we all say:
'She is dead.'

'Place two fingers of each hand beneath the body,' intones Lydia. Heads bowed, we are focused on our task.

'She is flying!'

We lift our fingers, slowly, without effort. Jill – all fifteen stone of her – rises into the air as if on a fork-lift truck. Lydia passes her hand to and fro beneath Jill's floating back. We don't dare breathe, or believe our eyes, or break the spell. My fingers fizz: Beelzebub brushes past, shaking the branches, scattering the birds. A whiff of burnt offerings, of incense.

And then Jill's sitting up, rubbing her eyes. 'Did it work?' she asks, yawning.

We're rolling on the grass, gasping and laughing, scared witless. Far below, the ground rumbles. The Northern line, or fiends from the deep?

Blame My Generation

The Oval, Kennington, London SE11

Just say 1971 and I'm back there at the end of a long hot summer, in my new purple-velvet flared hipsters. Down two whole sizes to a 12 – the reward of all that hyper-dieting, losing 15 pounds in 15 days. I'm feeling fantastic: edgy and elated.

Jill has wheedled tickets off her older brothers and we're going to the concert for Bangladesh. Mum banned us from going to Pink Floyd on Hampstead Heath, so this time I lied – I mean, I'm 18 and leaving for uni soon. She's clueless and this is fun.

I'm wearing no bra under my scoop-neck Indian top with little mirrors. It feels cool and sexy, I keep telling myself, trying to ignore the sweaty blokes leering at my tits on the long grimy Tube journey.

It's a massive gig: The Who and America and The Faces. The heat is stifling, and the sports ground is packed with thousands of hippy types. Jill wears black, slinky and glitzy; her blond hair sparkles in the sun, her feisty attitude crushing all the rude remarks about her size.

She's more daring than I'll ever be. Come on, skinny, she says, pulling me into the dancing. The noise is deafening, mind-blowing. Now The Who are smashing up their guitars on stage between arrays of monster speakers.

And this bloke comes up to her – a nasty little weasel with chipped teeth – and he says *wanna score* and she goes *ok* and I back off and he gives her a blue crystal tab of acid but I won't touch it and soon she's high as a kite and we're both bopping like crazy and everyone's whirling about with their arms in the air and the ground's dusty and the music's under my skin I wish it was Santana and I love my purple flares and I'm sweating everywhere and the little Indian mirrors are making crazy patterns in the sky . . .

and hours later we've collapsed back in the Tube ears buzzing legs tingling adrenaline racing –
and then Jill howls and she's crawling on the filthy seats and trying to get out of the blackened windows she's crying and wailing and I'm scared so absolutely shit-scared she's coming down she's in a real downer and everyone's gawping and I don't know what to do

all I can see is my mother shaking her head at me with such disappointment, her lips clamped shut.

No man's land

7km beyond Bab-e-Khyber, Pakistan*

Vultures rising on thermals, silhouettes in the white sky; their cries, and the odd ping of a falling pebble, are the only sounds. The sun has shrunk my shadow into a small bulbous Michelin-man.

No colours except bleached browns, greys, slender black shadows. No sign of Chuchi.

The empty road snakes up through barren cliffs, out of sight around sharp bends dynamited into rock. It comes back into view in the shimmering distance, a white band slicing across the mountainside, leaking rock falls.

I started out marching, now I'm stumbling in semi-panic, heart bouncing against my chest out of sync with the rucksack on my back. Abandoned by boyfriend. Some holiday.

The road surface is like a mirror, or mercury. It edges away from me; there's no water, no let-up to the sweat itching its way down my back and between my breasts. I'm breathing in time with my footsteps, noisily. Wet curtains of hair stick to my face.

The sound of tiny, distant bells reaches me: there are other people here? Far below, a herd of goats, finding their way over the scree, ambling or skipping.

Note to self: be more like goats.

I'm trying to see what's up the road. Is that gleam a metal roof, a sentry post?

Another dust-puff off a nearby rock; again, the distinctive ping. The penny drops. Adrenalin jumps me into a run – I'm laughing, singing out loud, that's no pebble, baby, let's not be 18 with a bullet, let's not get kyboshed up the Khyber, let's get to Afghanistan.

I have wings.

* The FATA (Federally Administered Tribal Area) between Landi Kotal in Pakistan and Torkham on the Pakistani border with Afghanistan. 'Far too dangerous for most travellers.' (Wikitravel)

Happy endings

Manchester and London

TELEGRAM: FATHER IN ACCIDENT STOP PHONE HOME SOONEST STOP MA

I'm shivering in the draughty piss-stinking phone-box; it's wintry in Chorlton-cum-Hardy and I hadn't put a coat on when I came out and made a reverse-charge call. I've been picking at faded cards stuck above the battered phone unit: handwritten statements such as 'French Lessens by Strict Teatcher' or 'discrete understanding Blond' and a phone number. Dad would love these, I'm thinking, he'd be in his element, correcting. They'd make him laugh.

I'm in the doorway to the ward at St George's. A sling suspends my father between bottles of yellow fluids. His face is grey, unshaven. I come closer. His eyes open; he blinks.

'Hello Shrimp,' he says hoarsely. Gurgled breathing. 'Bit of a prang. Doctors are bloody marvellous.'

I'm dutifully kissing him. Black blood crusts his jaw and chest.

'Hang on, Shrimp, I'll get you a cup of tea.' He waves at a bare wall; the dressing on his arm is stained with browns and reds. His eyes close again.

My mother appears, her arms open. 'How did your exam go?'
'Bit of a blur.' Who knew you needed statistics for a psychology degree?

A doctor has stepped into the doorway. 'He tripped over a shoelace,' he's saying. 'Crowded platform, the Victoria line. Extraordinary that he survived. The tube hit him full on.'

I'm nodding like one of those car toys.

Behind us, Dad's voice: 'Biscuit? Ask that pretty blonde nurse. Bet she knows her ginger nuts.'

'Has a psychiatrist seen him?' It seems an obvious question.

'No, he's perfectly lucid, gave them his home number and next-of-kin at the scene. Seriously, you're all so lucky.' The doctor stares at me, then at Mum. His smile fades.

I speak to him as if to a child. 'They've been divorced eight years. No shoelace involved.'

Not

St George's Hospital, Hyde Park Corner, London SW1

He's not hanging in a tangle of hooks and pulleys
No purple bruises on his face
No arm plastered no pelvis encased in bandages

I'm not shocked walking into the soulless hospital ward
My nostrils are not twitching with odours of
Disinfectant and morphine and despair and death

His voice does not croak out a faux-cheery greeting
Belying the seriousness of his injuries
The doctors have not denied his mental state

My mother is not estranged from him
She has not refused to accompany me
I'm not twenty-one
Not missing my sister

Dad has not jumped under a train

Postcards to my mother, 1974

USA

Dearest Ma, day one in New York: artists chalking Mona Lisa on the sidewalks, "Nixon Now" posters in the gutter, guys propositioning me on Broadway – do I look like a hooker? Holding a big pretzel? Went to Butch Cassidy and the Sundance Kid, Americana in the heart of America. I cried. Homesick. Luv V.

Dear Ma, I phoned Uncle Walter in Washington, he said come to his office – I arrived at the Pentagon in denim with rucksack. Driving home (limo/chauffeur) to Virginia, he said he'd expected someone more "British"! His wife assumed I'd "visit" for weeks, she'd organised meet-and-greet coffee mornings. TV on all day. Sorry, I just couldn't. Luv V.

Dear Ma, Onboard Greyhound at the New Jersey Turnpike. Go put on Simon&Garfunkel's 'America' right now, I'm watching crawling traffic in the rain, just like they sing. Going so far west I'll cross time zones! I'm feeling high (not like that!), lonely, alive. Can't wait to see Ian in SLC, 3 days. Luv V.

Dear Ma, Weird: Ian has a live-in girlfriend, never mentioned in his letters! We chatted for hours – she got bored+went off to bed after the pizza – he and I cuddled on the rug – you know I always had a crush on him. He played Pink Floyd's whole Dark Side of the Moon – must buy when I get home! Big row next day – I'm back on the bus. Luv V.

Hey Ma, Money arrived, thanks!! ♥ x Thing is, I met a guy in Hollywood – he stole my stuff etc. Too freaked out to contact Aunt Monica. Went south. In Laredo, this cowboy drawled, 'Y'all don't come from round here.' Understatement! Travelling alone=I can be anyone, different with everyone I meet – no one's checking, no one knows me. Might cross the border. Don't worry, I'm in my element. Reading Fear of Flying. V.

Hex

53 Hillway

'*Ach du lieber Himmel*, Hannah,' comes my mother's voice. 'How can you be so gullible?'

I can hear them out in the garden. I open my bedroom window a bit wider. They don't notice.

'But that's what it said in *The Guardian*, Ushi,' protests the guest. 'Those girls raided the infirmary for indigestion tablets –'
'Rubbish!' cuts in my mother. 'They were looking for quinine to induce abortions, obviously.'
'You can't be serious, Ushi,' says the other guest. 'In a *boarding* school?'

On the garden table stands the cafetière of strong coffee, a bowl of whipped double cream, demerara sugar cubes, the green-and-white Villeroy & Boch china, and a warmed-up oblong of shop-bought Danish pastry, still in its foil casing.

Home from uni, I'd crept upstairs to avoid my mother's regular *Kaffeeklatsch*.

'I should know, I used it often enough during the war,' continues my mother. Then, with a hollow laugh. 'Believe me, the institution is irrelevant.'

So. Just like that. She killed my brothers and sisters.

And what about me?

English

53 Hillway

Elsie is abrasive. And she barely talks to me – more often, she talks over me. She's not my favourite of Ursula's friends.

I'm back for a couple of weeks over the Easter holidays.

'Viv's got a boyfriend now, you know.' Ursula's pouring lapsang souchong into brown Denby cups.

Perched on the kitchen counter, now that I'm a topic of conversation, I stop trying to find Capital Radio. Elsie swivels to eyeball me.

'A boyfriend, even you! Is he English?'

I wonder if Ursula has told her the saga of my Turk, our trip overland from India and so on.

'Yes, this one's English.'

'I mean, is he really English?'

'Why wouldn't he be?' I sense I'm not following Elsie's codes, her semiotics.

Ursula puts down her cup. 'Well, I don't think Alan's Jewish, is he?'

'No, god no, he was in the Boy's Brigade, Methodist Sunday school and all that.'

'Quite right, good. And you're serious, the two of you?' Elsie's eyes drill into mine. I'm unnerved by how tea and chit-chat have somehow swerved into something of relevance to her.

I feel myself flush. So uncool. 'We're living together, so I suppose you could say – '

Elsie has turned away from me to accost Ursula and the teapot. She stretches out a hand weighed down with hefty, valuable rings. 'Marry out! That's the thing to do. Marry out and forget about it all. The whole verkakte mess.'

Patterns

53 Hillway

No manners, says one
she can't marry him, says the other
mother and grandmother
muttering together
over kitchen coffee
but they're blind and deaf to
what's obvious to me
Opa (Richard) proposed to Oma
pre-First World War
in some fairy-tale Heidi-hotel
in the Swiss Engadine
It was meant to be.
Dad (Richard) met Mum
post-Second World War
in a thunderstorm in the middle
of Lac Léman near Geneva
It was meant to be.
My boyfriend (Richard) proposed to me
after our student performance
of Verdi's Requiem
look at the history
How it's meant to be.
I'll ignore the dictatorial part
of their characters
I'm sure I can tame my Richard
whatever they say
I'll show them
not listening to them
It was meant to be.
It's all meant to be.

The gift

53 Hillway

SETTING: THE DINING ROOM, CHRISTMAS EVE, 1978, EVENING

Tree: red candles, unlit. Sconce wall lights in pairs, some not working. The Swingle Singers Christmas album plays on the old turntable. Roasting smells. A black-and-white cat.

Table: underpopulated despite white cloth, crystal glasses, best silver, lit candles. On each ornate porcelain plate: two slices melba toast, butter, parsley sprig, heaped grey bubbles.

GRANDMOTHER: angora, diamonds, pearls.
MOTHER: apron, twinset.
DAUGHTER: knit dress, heels.
DAUGHTER'S LIVE-IN BOYFRIEND: cheap suit.

MOTHER
(handing a bottle of Moet & Chandon to BOYFRIEND)
You're our token man. Mr Mikhailov next door gave me a bottle of vodka and a huge jar of caviar, would you believe it?

GRANDMOTHER
Quite extraordinary. Very kind of him.

MOTHER
I thought we'd better eat it. *(She swats the cat off her chair)* Saukater!

GRANDMOTHER
Be careful! She'll throw it down.

BOYFRIEND
Amazing! I've never tried caviar before.

MOTHER
Nor me, horrid idea, fish eggs. Do let's sit.

With beginner's luck, BOYFRIEND pops and pours the
champagne without mishap. The older women scrutinise him.

>   MOTHER
> It's Beluga, best in the world, he said.
>   GRANDMOTHER
> Who?
>   MOTHER
> The Russian.
>   GRANDMOTHER
> Oh. I thought he was a spy.
>   MOTHER
> I made the melba toast myself, d'you see? You toast a slice,
> cut it in half lengthwise, toast it again.
>   DAUGHTER
> Pretty butter curls.
>   MOTHER
> Oma made those.
>   GRANDMOTHER
> The maids in my house at Wachwitz had proper butter
> curlers. I had to take a teaspoon.

DAUGHTER sees BOYFRIEND hesitate; she picks up her toast; all
follow; they take a first bite.

>   BOYFRIEND
> Ooh, strange.
>   DAUGHTER
> Bursts on your tongue, doesn't it?
>   MOTHER
> Fishy –
>   BOYFRIEND
> Delicious!

DAUGHTER

Mmm!

MOTHER

Thank heaven we have the pheasant.

GRANDMOTHER

Dreadfully fishy.

MOTHER

Pfui Deibel! I can't eat it.

GRANDMOTHER

Quite awful. *(She takes a long sip of champagne, puts her glass down carefully, smooths her napkin)* Ghastly.

The music has stopped. A dramatic pause. DAUGHTER snorts, shoulders shaking, mouth full. BOYFRIEND sees her face, starts laughing. MOTHER's eyes crinkle, she loses control, giggles hysterically. The cat stretches.

MOTHER

Oh dear. Dear me.

GRANDMOTHER

What's so funny?

MOTHER *(Manages to blurt)*

I'm afraid the caviar got the better of me.

GRANDMOTHER *(Deadpan)*

Very much the better.

Cat approaches.

BLACKOUT.

Item 18: 'Angel chimes' Swedish Christmas rotating mobile table centrepiece, polished brass angel cut-outs.

Sharper than a serpent's tooth

Harrow, Middlesex

SETTING: EXT./INT. WINTER, 1980s, DAY

DAUGHTER parks outside a drab block of flats. Council workers are digging up the road. Inside the flat: bachelor chaos, mouldy smells. She stands in the middle of the cramped living room, jacket over arm.

> FATHER *(Slumped in his decrepit soft chair)*
> Bonjour old thing! Is it Wednesday already? That's when *(Mockney accent)* me so-shall woiker comes – to check Oi 'aven't hexpired. I've got through a few of them *(Laughs uproariously)*. This one's Brenda or perhaps it's Sally. The meek little-woman type, but when I asked her what authors she's read, she said she liked detective thrillers, strewth, fancy that!

Drilling outside.

> *(He doesn't pause)* This one's not too bad, she's quite a game bird – in a nice plum-coloured coat with a rather flashy handbag. Flat shoes – why on earth would any woman except a nurse wear flat shoes? Unbecoming, the ankles aren't shown off properly. She wears that terrible turquoise eye makeup. Well, sit down.
>
> Your mother – never needed makeup and what a figure, eh? Would've made a marvellous artist's model!

Brief silence outside. DAUGHTER edges stack of newspapers off stool, sits.

> I can't bear a certain type of woman – Elizabeth Taylor,

Jackie Onassis – with a great gash of a mouth covered in lipstick, brows painted on, hideous.

Fancy some Stilton? *(Indicates kitchen counter;* DAUGHTER *doesn't look)* You can scrape the mould off.

DAUGHTER leans forward in an attempt to speak.

(He keeps talking) No, I haven't seen Sally – or is it Brenda? – lately. Last time I invited her for a cup of tea and a biscuit and she rather reluctantly joined me. Didn't know where to put herself. No idea how to have a normal conversation.

Drilling resumes. DAUGHTER stands, puts on jacket.

Well, yes, I suppose she has to do her job, buggered if I know what it is. D'you really have to go already?

BLACKOUT.

Visiting hours

Les Eaux Vives, Brussels, Belgium

The double-doors let me into the hot-house ambiance of the *résidence*. In the sober vestibule, the matron intercepts me, scanning me with overt disapproval.

'And who are you precisely?' she asks.
My best French. 'My grandmother, Madame Vollmann, is unwell.'
'Indeed, nobody informed me.'

The smartly dressed woman conducts me into the lift and up to the first floor. I expect to find my 93-year-old grandmother tucked up in bed with a nurse on call. But as we emerge into the carpeted corridor, her diminutive figure – coiffed hair, tailored silk dress – is standing on the threshold of her apartment.

'Madame Vollmann, so you're in poor health, are you?'
'Who's been telling tales?' A glare at me.
'But you didn't notify me of your condition, Madame Vollmann.'
'That is none of your business, frankly, Madame!'

The matron turns and walks away.

'Well since you're here, I suppose it could be time for coffee.' Oma goes in; I follow.

I'm on the sofa, china cup-and-saucer balanced over my swollen belly. From her upright chair, Oma blinks as if noticing me for the first time.
'You are pale, child. Are you getting enough vitamins?'

Naturally I'm pale, you silly old woman, shouts the Voice in my Head. *I'm seven months pregnant and I've had a horrible flight to Brussels, I've abandoned my two small boys with their useless dad –*

'I'm fine, Oma,' says the Voice in my Mouth. 'I've come to fill in for my mother.'

I give a bright, forced laugh.

'Oh well, your *mother*,' says my grandmother with a Gallic shrug, 'she's *never* there when I need her.'
'But Oma, Mum's on one of her long guiding tours.' A sip of coffee, so strong that I shudder. 'I'm sure she'll get in touch as soon as she can.'
'That's no good at all,' declares Oma. 'It's *now* I want her. We have things to discuss, important things.'

You ungrateful cow! says the Voice in my Head. *You frightened me, phoning to yammer how ailing you were – it was five in the morning! I didn't know where Mum and her group were staying in Bournemouth. And when I finally found her she told me she couldn't stop halfway through the tour. You really worried her, you selfish old –*

'Well, Oma, now you've got me. Here I am, to help,' I say.

'*You?*' My grandmother scowls at me. 'What an idea.' She continues, 'If you'd like to put your feet up – gracious, they are puffy, aren't they? – I've got a lot to do: I must phone Mme Rolland about things I need, and then I have some letters to write, to the bank, and the Berlin cousins . . .'
I sleep poorly in the visitor room, a hideous, long-ago feeling dragging at me. I stay only one night.

My baby kicks all through the flight back to London.

Social comedy sleeper
(according to *The New York Times* **review**)

53 Hillway

SETTING: AT THE KITCHEN TABLE, 1985, DAY

Same old brown Denby teapot, fragrant scent of Lapsang Souchong tea, no milk. VIVIAN visiting.

URSULA

My friend Elsa and I went to that new film, the one everyone's talking about.

VIVIAN

Elsa who?

URSULA

Oh she's *so* much fun, we have an absolute hoot together! We've been to lots of exhibitions and she doesn't mekker about her health or her children. I left the car in Tufnell Park and took the Tube to Finchley; it was on at that cinema you recommended. It really was shocking!

VIVIAN

The Phoenix? Hang on, I don't know which film you mean.

URSULA

You know, the queer one.

VIVIAN

Not sure –

URSULA

– with the young man who gets picked up, terribly gritty. *The Laundry.*

VIVIAN *(Rolls eyes)*

No idea.

URSULA

Oh come on! There's such a kerfuffle about it! I don't mind

the idea but I don't want to see men kissing and I had to close my eyes, disgusting! They had sex, you know, they buggered each other!

VIVIAN *(Leafing through 'Time Out')*

Oh wait, is it *My Beautiful Laundrette*?

URSULA

Well, we left. Couldn't stand it. Elsa whispered, 'Are you enjoying this?' and I said 'No, I've got my eyes shut!' so we crept out. *(Laughs, tears come to her creased-up eyes, she's close to hysteria)* We had to sneak out like silly schoolgirls but it was awful! *(Her own firm voice calms her)* Men can do what they like in private but I don't want to watch a whole film about it, with them doing it, really fucking! *(Her voice is loud but once she's said it, her vehemence goes)*

VIVIAN

It's revolutionary and ground-breaking –

URSULA *(Mildly)*

Well yes, quite right. I suppose your father should go.

VIVIAN *(Laughs)*

You're joking! He hates gays, he's always ranting about them –

URSULA *(Quietly)*

His proclivities, you know.

BLACKOUT.

I fear that this batch of porridge is now inedible.
I fear that these bloody homosexuals, degenerates, officials,
nit-picking pen-pushing snotty little men, these interfering
harridans, these idiot bank clerks and illiterate long-haired shits
from some godforsaken council estate in Basingstoke who call up
and ask for Mr Thronger – these damned people will hound
me into my grave.
I fear that they are going to use electroshock therapy on me, again –
it's awful, they strap me down, the pain is terrible, please don't let
them, please call the director,
I beg you to stop them.

Letter from Harley Street
15th October '61 [copy found in boxed office archives, 1991]

Dear Larry,

I am dashing off a quick note to ask you for a second opinion on a patient, RT, whom I saw this morning. Not a regular, but someone to whom I was recommended by a mutual acquaintance, via the patient's wife.

They were shown in together, and Mrs T (vivacious, good figure, poss. continental) was forthcoming, worried that Mr T is sleeping poorly, not eating well etc. He sent her several black looks, so I asked her to wait outside and continued with RT alone. He initially spoke in monosyllables, answering questions curtly, but once our exchanges revealed certain similarities between us, conversation became easy and animated. Turns out he is a Cambridge man too, went up to Pembroke in '36, rowed Goldie to victory! Literature rather than medicine. Speaks several languages, lectures/writes on postwar foreign affairs. Keen on music (plays the piano), art, theatre etc., a man of many talents. Living just over the Heath - his daughters go to the same school as Emma.

His problem? He affected voices and accents at the drop of a hat, laughed, cracked jokes and showed every sign of mania. Admitted to the sleeplessness his wife mentioned, stating that it was due to his wife's mother trying to sabotage their marriage, as well as exert sinister influence on how he brings up his children. (One is asthmatic and he feels a fuss should not be made - as you know I have personal experience with all that.) The mother-in-law lives abroad so the fear of influence is patently redundant. I probed further about his parents and siblings (you and I are in agreement re: early-life incidents, parenting distance, incest, etc.), but he became withdrawn, with no further responses. When our time ran short and we stood to shake hands, he asked if I had a diagnosis. I replied in the affirmative, that he showed early signs of paranoid schizophrenia, and that his wife was right to be concerned. He said he would like a second opinion, and left rather agitated, not surprisingly. As he fetched their coats, I had a quick word with Mrs T in the waiting room, to let her know I would ask a colleague to oblige - I expect she will telephone to make an appointment in the next few days. Only fly in the ointment would be if her husband forbids her from doing so, but I believe trust has been established.

Once you have run your Jungian eye over him, I expect to see RT regularly. First thing is to control his symptoms with a good medication regime.

Yrs,

Tony

Dr Anthony Storr
MB BChir (Cantab), MRCP, DPM, FRCPsych

Filing note November 1962: Dr Storr's office has received no replies to letters, nor further communication from potential patient RT, nor did RT, or others on his behalf, make any contact with Dr L. It is assumed that RT has decided not to pursue private treatment.

Her shoes III

The Highgate Care Home, 12 Hornsey Lane, London N6

Her swollen feet are pressed into low-heeled, navy-blue court shoes with an ornamental buckle of conjoined silver Cs; the soles are barely scuffed. Incongruous support tights – brown, sagging, gleaming with elastane – have been paired with these trophy shoes, bought from an elegant Brussels branch of Bally, at the end of a leisurely sales process during which Madame had been offered coffee and a seat on a white sofa. Although out of place within the trappings of modern terminal care, the shoes are too ladylike to complain, and are glad for this brief, last outing.

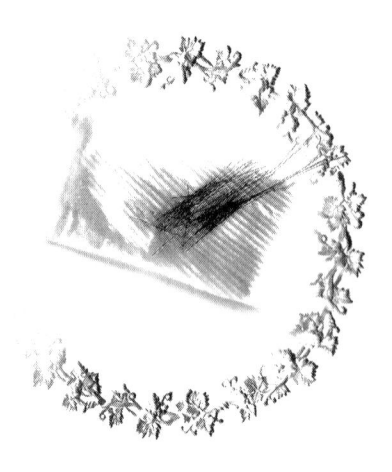

Item 19: Wedgwood Blue Jasperware butter dish with lid;
unsalted butter; trapped cat hairs

EPILOGUE

The same river twice

53 Hillway

'Come sit,' says our mother after Oma's funeral.

'There's something I want to show you both.
In case you think, someday, we should have discussed this.
In case you can't remember whether we discussed this.
In case you're reminded of things your parents talked about, one day.
In case you're reminded of things your grandparents said.
The only constant thing is change, they used to say.
So, in case there's a change in politics. There will be.
In case you ever find yourself looking for paperwork.
In case you find yourself looking at paperwork.
In case your children ask about heritage.
In case questions come up about your children's heritage.
In case they ever ask about the German side.
In case they ask about the other German side.
In case you ever need to show official documents.
In case they don't ask about the Lutheran church.
In case you need proof that your grandmother was baptised.
In case you ever need to prove you're not Jews. Yes, you two.
In case it ever happens again.'

'Take it.' She unfolds a brittle document.
We hesitate. She holds it out. 'Just in case.'

Item 20: Stone 'country boy' garden statue, 1.5m, French or German, 18th-century costume, tricorn hat, holding fruit basket, some damage

POSTSCRIPT

Letters from the dead

Eva and Dick Vollmann (Oma and Opa) were divorced in 1938 by Nazi decree (the Aryan Marriage laws classed all marriages between Jews and non-Jews as illegal).

Eva then fled to South America while Dick remained in Germany. To avoid suspicion with the authorities, Dick remarried.

After the war, the two continued their close contact and correspondence until Dick's death in 1966.

Their letters have been translated from the original German (by CT) and are edited.

NOTES

Discography

'Dicky Bird Hop' by Ron Gourley, sung by Ann Stephens, from the 1941 4-song recording *Children's Choice*

'Das ist die Berliner Luft' by Paul Lincke, sung by Lizzy Waldmüller in the 1941 movie *Frau Luna*

'Black Bottom' by de Sylva/Brown/Henderson, vocal version by Bob Crosby and his orchestra, 1950

'The Gas-Man Cometh' by Flanders and Swann, 1960

'Mackie Messer (Mack the Knife)' by Weill/Brecht, sung by Hildegard Knef, 1963

Frankie and Johnny' trad. USA, adapted and sung by Josh White, 1946

'Joshua' trad. slave spiritual, sung by Odetta, 1956

'Banana Boat (Day O)' trad. Jamaican, sung by Harry Belafonte from his 1956 album *Calypso*

'De Hamborger Veermaster (The Hamburg Four-master)' trad. German sea shanty, sung by Freddy, 1961

'I Hold Your Hand in Mine' by Tom Lehrer from his 1953 album *Songs by Tom Lehrer*

'Cocktails for Two' by Johnston/Coslow, performed by Spike Jones and his City Slickers, 1945

'Phonetic Punctuation' by Victor Borge, from his 1955 album *Victor Borge: Phonetic Punctuation*

'The Little White Duck' by Zaritsky/Barrows, sung by Burl Ives on the 1950 album *Burl Ives Sings Little White Duck and Other Children's Favorites*

'Aquarius'/Let the Sunshine In (The Flesh Failures)' by Rado/Radni/MacDermot, sung by the original Broadway cast of *Hair,* 1968

Reference

'Headbangers': Attarian, H. et al, *Journal of Clinical Sleep Medicine,* published online 15.12.2009.

First published

'Her Shoes I/II/III': A combined version titled 'Triptych: her shoes' appeared in *BONSAI: Best small stories from Aotearoa New Zealand*, eds. Michelle Elvy, Frankie McMillan and James Norcliffe, Canterbury University Press 2018.

'Not': Shortlisted in the NZ NFFD *Micro Madness* competition, and published online in June 2021.

'Precious': An earlier version was published online in the June 2016 edition of *Flash Frontier.*

'Prickly': A version in the form of a poem titled 'Prickly Heat' appeared in *Offshoots 11* published 2011 by Geneva Writers' Group.

'Sick day': A version was shortlisted and published online in the 2017 NZ NFFD *Tiny Tales* competition, and was awarded the Best Northland Short Story prize.

'The Great Outdoors': A fiction version titled 'Reservoir' appeared in *Offshoots 14* published 2017 by Geneva Writers' Group.

'Weight': An earlier version was published online in May 2016 in *Writers Up North.*

'Years passed, and the front door still stuck': A version titled 'Years passed, we never mowed the lawn and the front door still stuck' was shortlisted in the NZ NFFD *Micro Madness* competition, and published online in June 2021.